rororo sprachen
Herausgegeben von Ludwig Moos

Geschäftsbesuche im Ausland sind für internationale Kontakte selbstverständlich. Zwar wird Englisch überall als Business-Sprache verwendet, doch halten die kulturellen Eigenheiten der jeweiligen Länder jede Menge sprachlicher und praktischer Fallen bereit. *Let's Go International* begleitet ein junges Verkaufstalent rund um die Welt und beschreibt die Schwierigkeiten, die es zu meistern hat. Mit Sinn für Situationskomik wird in einer lockeren Mischung aus Dialogen und Übungen der Blick geschärft für die traditionellen Vorurteile und für die Fettnäpfchen, die es zu vermeiden gilt, wenn die Geschäfte gelingen sollen. Die Toncassette zum Buch (60508) verrät, wie sich das alles anhört, und schult im Sprechen.

Dr. René Bosewitz ist native speaker und unterrichtet an der Berufsakademie Mannheim. In einer deutschen Zweigstelle der London Chamber of Commerce bereitet er Firmenangehörige auf einschlägige sprachliche Prüfungen vor. Er trainiert zudem seit vielen Jahren Manager aus Banken und Industrie in Business English. Mit Robert Kleinschroth hat er bei rororo sprachen *Joke Your Way Through English Grammar* (8527) und *Joke by Joke to Conversation* (8797) veröffentlicht.

Robert Kleinschroth unterrichtet Englisch am Gymnasium und an der Universität Heidelberg. Er hat zwanzig Jahre Praxis in der Erwachsenenbildung und leitete fünfzehn Jahre lang die Sprachabteilung eines Großunternehmens.
Robert Kleinschroth hat zusammen mit Dieter Maupai *La Grammaire en s'amusant* (8714) verfaßt und *La Conversation en s'amusant* (8873) sowie *Sprachen lernen* (9140) und *Neues Lernen mit dem Computer* (9841) geschrieben.

In der Reihe *Business English* sind von beiden Autoren außerdem erschienen: *Manage in English* (60137), *How to Phone Effectively* (60139), *Better than the Boss* (60138), *Test Your Management Skills* (60260) und *Get Through at Meetings* (60262)

RENÉ BOSEWITZ / ROBERT KLEINSCHROTH

LET'S GO INTERNATIONAL

BUSINESS ENGLISH RUND UM DIE WELT

Rowohlt

Impressum

Wir danken Frau Ortrud Grimm vielmals
für ihre Hilfe bei der Erstellung des Manuskripts.
Ohne sie hätten wir es wohl nicht geschafft.

Originalausgabe
Veröffentlicht im
Rowohlt Taschenbuch Verlag GmbH,
Reinbek bei Hamburg, September 1997
Copyright © 1997 by
Rowohlt Taschenbuch Verlag GmbH,
Reinbek bei Hamburg
Umschlaggestaltung Barbara Hanke
(Illustration Cathrin Günther)
Textillustrationen Christian Mentzel
Layout Alexander Urban
Satz PostScript OCR-A und Stone,
QuarkXPress 3.31 (Dolev 800)
Druck und Bindung Clausen & Bosse, Leck
Printed in Germany
1690-ISBN 3 499 60267 9

Inhalt

Vorwort	6
Gebrauchsanweisung	8

1	**Focus on the USA (1):** It all begins in America	11
2	**Focus on the USA(2):** Making friends the American way	23
3	**Focus on Britain (1):** One language – two minds	35
4	**Focus on Britain (2):** Golf clubs for the temperamental player	49
5	**Focus on Ireland:** Balls with a beep	61
6	**Focus on Germany (1):** Filling in forms in Frankfurt	73
7	**Focus on Germany (2):** Beeping balls for the Board	85
8	**Focus on Portugal:** Big deal with Sporty-Rest	97
9	**Focus on Spain:** Boards and rods for the weak	109
10	**Focus on France:** Splitting hairs in Strasburg	123
11	**Focus on Russia:** Building bridges in Moscow	137
12	**Focus on Saudi Arabia:** Balls and clubs for combat packs	149
13	**Focus on Japan (1):** Will we ever understand the Japanese?	161
14	**Focus on Japan (2):** Sports articles for the undersized	169
15	**Focus on China (1):** The Chinese connection	179
16	**Focus on China (2):** Singing balls and propaganda	189
17	**Focus on South-America:** Love's labour lost in Mexico?	199

Key to the exercises	208
Key to the crossword puzzles	232
Glossary	236
Sources	248

Vorwort

James Kelly verkauft so nützliche Dinge wie Mountainbikes für Asthmatiker, Golfbälle mit eingebautem Piepser, Tennis- und Golfschläger, die dank elektronischen Schnickschnacks dem Stubenhocker zur sportlichen Eleganz des Profis verhelfen.

Als typischer profitorientierter Amerikaner hat er es auf seinen Geschäftsreisen nicht leicht. Jede Nation hat ihre eigenen Fettnäpfchen ausgelegt. Viele Politiker und Manager kehren daher ohne Ergebnisse von einer Auslandsmission zurück. Bob Kohls, Direktor des Washington International Center, schätzt, daß jährlich rund 80 Prozent der amerikanischen Geschäftsleute unverrichteter Dinge wieder nach Hause fahren. Sie verstehen es nicht, in einem fremden Kulturkreis erfolgreich zu verhandeln. Erinnern Sie sich? Ein großer deutscher Elektrokonzern gefährdete kürzlich einen Auftrag von über 150 Millionen, weil er durch Zusammenarbeit mit einem zwielichtigen Agenten den nationalen Stolz der Kolumbianer verletzte. Doch zusammen mit James Kelly werden Sie lernen, wie und wann Visitenkarten und Gastgeschenke in Saudi-Arabien, China und Japan zu überreichen sind, in welchem Land man engen Körper- und Blickkontakt erwartet und wo man auf Distanz zu gehen hat. Was bedeutet es, wenn man in China die Eßstäbchen fallen läßt, in einem arabischen Land die Fußsohlen nicht verbirgt, in Portugal rote Nelken, in China einen Tirolerhut überreicht? Sind es die Chinesen, denen man nicht in die Augen schauen sollte, oder sind es die Araber? Wie verhält man sich, wenn die japanischen Partner bei Präsentationen beharrlich schweigen oder gar zu schlafen scheinen?

Die *business etiquette* läßt sich lernen. Viel schwieriger ist es, sich den unterschiedlichen Verhandlungsstrategien anzupassen, die auf anderen Denkweisen und Werteskalen beruhen. Wußten Sie, daß selbst in Europa Italiener, Spanier, Deutsche und Briten etwas anderes unter Wahrheit oder der Gültigkeit von Verträgen verstehen? Wo betont man die Qualität seiner Produkte, und wo streicht man besser die Qualitäten seiner Persönlichkeit heraus? James Kelly denkt geradlinig, Schritt für Schritt. Spanier und Araber sind häufig mit mehreren

Dingen gleichzeitig befaßt, Russen, Chinesen und Japaner verhandeln wieder ganz anders.

Mit diesem Buch wollen wir Ihnen helfen, Mißerfolge zu vermeiden und gleichzeitig Ihre Sprachkompetenz auszubauen. Dabei bleiben wir der Devise unserer *Business English*-Reihe treu, Lernen mit Ironie und Witz schmackhaft zu machen. Begleiten Sie James Kelly auf seiner Geschäftsreise quer durch die Welt. Seine Vorurteile und die daraus entstehenden Schwierigkeiten werden Sie für die kulturellen Unterschiede in der Geschäftswelt sensibilisieren. Wir haben dabei Eigenheiten der Völker übertrieben und verallgemeinert, nicht weil wir an nationale Stereotype glauben, sondern weil wir Unterschiede verdeutlichen wollten, von denen wir meinen, daß sie typisch sind. Natürlich gibt es den Amerikaner oder den Deutschen ebensowenig wie den Spanier oder den Japaner.

Vergebens haben wir nach Vorbildern für mögliche Übungen gesucht, die *cross-cultural awareness* und Verhandlungstechniken zugleich schulen. Wir haben selber welche erfunden, einer Variante von James Kellys Wahlspruch folgend: KISS (Keep it Simple but Subtle). Die Übungen sind übersichtlich, kurz und schnell zu lösen. Allerdings erfordern sie ein genaues Lesen der Dialoge. Und wenn Sie wissen wollen, wie es klingt, wählen Sie die Ausgabe mit der Audio-CD oder kaufen die Tonkassette zum Buch. Kursleiter oder Lehrer werden die abwechslungsreichen Übungsformen mit Gewinn in den Unterricht einbringen. Wir wünschen Ihnen viel Spaß und Erfolg.

Gebrauchsanweisung

Jedes Kapitel ist einer Nation, die mitunter auch für einen Kulturkreis steht, gewidmet. Dieser Überblick über markante „Etappen" auf der Reise in das Zielland wird Ihnen bei der Lektüre helfen.

The Story: Die Erfahrungen von James Kelly mit Geschäftspartnern in aller Welt sind Ausgangspunkt für die Übungen eines Kapitels. Viele Episoden haben wir vertont. Besitzen Sie die Buchausgabe mit Audio-CD oder haben Sie die Tonkassette dazugekauft, erzielen Sie den größten Lernerfolg, wenn Sie so vorgehen:

1. Sie lesen den Dialog.
2. Sie hören und lesen mit.
3. Sie hören ohne den Text.
4. Sie beantworten die Fragen von *Train your brain (Task 1)*, die in jedem Kapitel unmittelbar auf den Dialog folgen.
5. Sie machen die Übungen, die wir Ihnen zu der Audioversion anbieten.

Vocabulary to help you with the texts: Die Wortschatzliste sorgt dafür, daß Sie beim Lesen, Hören und Üben alles verstehen. Sie hilft Ihnen auch bei der Lösung der *crossword puzzles* zu vielen der besuchten Länder.

Time for a smile, Food for thought, Hit them on the head: Humor wird bei uns groß geschrieben. Ausgesuchte Witze und geistreiche Zitate zum Thema sorgen dafür, daß Sie bei der Lektüre das Lächeln nicht vergessen. *Hit them on the head* sind Spöttereien aus dem Munde berühmter Persönlichkeiten, spitzfindige Vorurteile mit einem Körnchen Wahrheit, mit denen alle Nationen zu leben haben. In den Briefen, die James Kelly nach Hause schickt, oder in seinen Tagebuchaufzeichnungen spiegeln sich diese Vorurteile etwas derber.

(M) Mind your manners: In übersichtlicher Form haben wir zusammengestellt, worauf die Menschen des jeweiligen Landes besonders empfindlich reagieren – Themen, die tabu sind.

(L) Going international: Gegen Ende eines jeden Kapitels faßt ein Lesetext weitere Besonderheiten der betreffenden *business culture* zusammen, um die der Geschäftsmann wissen muß, soll seine Reise in das andere Land von Erfolg gekrönt sein.

(B) Brainwork umfaßt meist vier bis sechs Übungstypen (*tasks*).

Train your brain: Diese Übung schult Ihr Lese- und Hörverstehen. Sie haben den Text gelesen (oder angehört). Nun testen wir mit Fragen zur *story* Ihr Gedächtnis. Diese Fragen sollten Sie sich auch nach Anhören des Dialogs von Kassette oder Audio-CD vornehmen.

Understanding American English: Amerikaner und Engländer verstehen sich zwar, aber sie sprechen nicht immer die gleiche Sprache. Die einschlägigen Übungen machen auf die Unterschiede in Wortschatz und Idiomatik aufmerksam und helfen, *the hidden message* zu verstehen.

Watch their ways: Andere Völker – andere Sitten. Wer auf internationalem Parkett nicht ausrutschen will, muß sein Bewußtsein für die *cross-cultural differences* schärfen. Wir haben sie in die Dialoge eingebaut, sie in Übersichten gefaßt oder sie mit amerikanischen beziehungsweise europäischen Denkweisen kontrastiert. Hier schärfen Sie Ihr Bewußtsein für die Empfindlichkeiten anderer Völker, vor allem aber lernen Sie die Gebote der nationalen *business etiquette* kennen.

Patchwork: Mit den *patches* des „Flickwerks" ergänzen Sie merkwürdige Redewendungen, die Sie mit dieser kurzen Übung vertiefen.

The travelling manager's country quiz: Hier kann der Geschäftsmann seine Kenntnisse über das Land auf unterhaltsame Weise testen und ergänzen.

Our country crossword puzzle: Das Kreuzworträtsel soll Wortschatz und Fakten des vorangegangenen Kapitels vertiefen. Der aufmerksame Leser wird keine Schwierigkeiten haben, es zu lösen.

Key to the exercises: Hier finden Sie nicht nur die Lösungen zu allen Aufgaben, sondern auch wertvolle Zusatzinformationen über die Geschäftskultur des betreffenden Landes.

Glossary: Hier finden Sie die alphabetische Liste der im Text erklärten Wörter.

FOCUS ON THE USA
Chapter 1
It all begins in America

🙂 Time for a smile

The American tourist is visiting a zoo in London. In front of the kangaroo house he stopped dead[1], still chewing[2]. Said he, "one thing I really grant[3] you, Brits[4]. Your grass-hoppers are really a lot bigger than ours back in Texas."

---

1 plötzlich anhalten 2 kauen 3 das muß man euch wirklich lassen 4 Briten

Chapter 1

Bring back that 'cabbage'

Our little story begins back in that most federal of countries, the USA. Born and bred in St. Paul, the capital of Minnesota, was ..., wait for it, Jamie. Or more correctly James Kelly the Second. You've guessed it. James Kelly the First, was his father. This father had been a successful businessman and top manager at a famous communication and office equipment company with a "three" in its name. James, the son, received the best that money could buy. High-school education, clothes, friends etc. A typical upper middle-class American. And, of course, he got a good job as a sales manager (with a little help from his dad). But what sort of company did he join?

The company? Well, it was certainly young (so was James), and perhaps a little naive and over-optimistic (just like James). And inexperienced (no comment). What about the products? Well, Sports Aids for the Slow Learner, or SASL for short, have many innovative ideas. They offer a product and a service. The product is a range of sports equipment which is designed in such a way that special things begin to happen if the learner does not play his shot correctly. These instruments are the "optimal" way to learn if you are not "hacked" from the same rock as the Gräfin, the Baker, Bernhardt Long, Genghis Khan, Michael Shoemaker and all the others.

> James is called to the office of his boss, Dave Makeit:
> James (J), Dave (D)

D: *(pumping James' hand and slapping him on the shoulder)*
Well, you did a great job this year, son. We've opened up markets all over the States. You're one in a thousand.

J: Oh, it was nothing, Dave. As my dad would say, "I'm a chip off the old block."

D: Well, I wouldn't exactly call your father an old block. Certainly he's not old.

J: Well, sir, he's about the same age as you, Dave.

D: I didn't bring you here to talk about age. Let's get to the point. I've got plans for you. You know where Europe is, don't you James?

J: Yeah, a bunch of states stuck together and located 2,000 miles off the east coast of the US.

FOCUS ON THE USA 1

D: You got it! Now I want you to go there and show those Europeans what made America great. Sell, sell, sell! And when you've conquered that market there's the Russians, the Arabs and the East.
J: I thought the Russians were European.
D: Only geographically. It's easy. The Europeans are our friends. The Russians aren't. So the Russians can't be Europeans. Piece of cake!
J: Got ya! When do I go?
D: This afternoon! Don't let the flies breed on you, or whatever the expression is.
J: I guess you mean "a rolling stone gathers no moss".
D: Music's not my thing. Selling sports equipment is. Now go for it, baby, and bring back that cabbage!
J: What are you talking about vegetables for?
D: Man, you upper-class dudes aren't in touch with the real world. Cabbage, loot, greenbacks, dollars, my friend, green gold.
J: Got ya! Money. I'm on my way. See ya.

Dear James, armed with maps, documents, samples and youthful self-confidence, sets off for England, a small country in the United Kingdom of Great Britain and Northern Ireland. With its 94,251 square miles it is slightly smaller than the US state of Oregon. All James knows about that place is that it is somewhere in Europe, a small continent just off the coast of America.

B Task 1: Train your brain

1. What does James Kelly sell?
    a communication and office equipment
    b all sorts of sports equipment
    c sports aids for the slow learner

2. What does SASL mean?
    a sports aid for super learners
    b sports aids for the slow learner
    c sports aid for smart learners

3. Where is James' home-town located?
    a on the fork of the Mississippi and Missouri Rivers
    b on the fork of the Mississippi and Minnesota Rivers
    c on the fork of the Mississippi and the Hudson Rivers

Chapter 1

B Task 2: Understanding the Americans (1)

Look at the text. What do these American phrases mean?

1. You got it!
   a You've already got it.
   b That's exactly right.
   c You're a clever guy.

2. Got ya!
   a I see what you mean.
   b My God!
   c You've got a yacht, haven't you?

3. Piece of cake!
   a Have a piece of cake!
   b What a nonsense!
   c It's as easy as that!

4. Bring back that cabbage!
   a Buy some cabbage!
   b You speak rubbish!
   c Fetch those dollars in!

B Task 3: Understanding the Americans (2)

Look again at the text and find the American English phrases.

A British person says	Our Americans have said
You've done a great job this year.	....
a group of neighbouring states	....
That's exactly right.	....
I see what you mean.	....
It's as easy as that!	....
I think ...	....
Music's not my cup of tea.	....
Fetch those dollars in!	....
bloke	....
my boy	....
See you!	....

FOCUS ON THE USA 1

Task 4: Watch their ways

Nations differ also regarding body contact. In East-European countries, for example, politicians hug and kiss each other. Look again at our dialogue. Can you find anything that is typically American?

Task 5 : Country quiz – American manners

Are the following statements true or false?   T F

Dave and James call each other by their first names. It is like saying *du* to someone in Germany.

D*ave:* You did a great job this year, son. You're one in a million. Is it true that Americans pay each other more compliments than Germans do?

Dave: The Europeans are our friends. The f...ing Russians aren't... Is it true that only very old-fashioned people will be shocked if you use so-called four letter words like shit, fuck in informal everyday conversation.

James: Well, *sir*, he's about the same age as you, Dave. Is it true that in everyday conversation "sir" is a form of respect?

☺ Time for a smile

James Kelly on his trip to Europe on Concorde was busy studying the ways and traditions of the European countries he was going to visit. As they were flying over Europe, the stewardess, in an attempt[1] to make the trip entertaining, said. "That's Paris down there, sir."
"Don't bother me with details", snapped[2] the executive. "Just mention the continents."

---
1 Versuch 2 anfahren, anschnauzen

Chapter 1

 Typical American: About bosses and time

1. I didn't bring you here to talk about age

Dave Makeit is a typical American boss. Just like many American bosses he sees himself in the role of a coach rather than a boss. However, there is a well-defined distance between both. Beneath the relaxed and familiar style and the ready use of first names, there is a strict code of manners. Like in football, the American coach gives more directions than advice. Both bosses and coaches manage and direct their teams during the course of a competition.

American bosses have not the reputation of being skilled or patient in dealing with arguments from their subordinates. Discussions are open to the point of being brusque. Bluntness is preferred to subtelty *(Man, you upper-class dudes aren't in touch with the real world)*. They tend to see disagreement as insubordination rather than constructive criticism. As Samuel Goldwyn once said: "I don't want any yes-men around me. I want everybody to tell me the truth – even if it costs them their jobs."

2. Don't let the flies breed on you

Time is money. The American is always on the go, always in a hurry, rarely stopping to enjoy the present – a slave to the clock. That is why he (or she) had to invent fast food and instant coffee. He treats time as a valuable and limited resource. Like money he saves it, wastes it, gives it, takes it, spends it, runs out of it and budgets it.

This affects his way of conducting business. He often lacks patience *(Let's get to the point.)* and will say provocative things to get things moving. Whether it is a job interview, sales call, or any other kind of business meeting, the American will be on time. To arrive early, however, would suggest that the caller has time to spare, an impression one would wish to avoid. A visitor in America will be kept waiting only briefly. A longer wait would communicate lack of interest. In Saudi Arabia the same manager would have to spend a couple of days in his hotel until the Saudi is ready to see him.

American managers have difficulties in adapting to business cultures where time is flexible, where drinking coffee and chatting is considered as doing something and not as a waste of time.

Adapted from Lennie Copeland, Lewis Griggs, *Going International*

FOCUS ON THE USA

 Going international: The flight

Do's

1. Membership in a frequent-flyer club: Since James Kelly will become a jet-setter he has joined a frequent-flyer programme to get special treatment. And indeed, he got a free ticket for Madame Tussaud's museum and a special price at the Hilton in London. If he does enough mileage he might even get a free flight home.

2. Ticketless boarding: James had his favourite seat reserved by phone. You show your indentity pass at the check-in and you get your boarding card. He asked for a discounted business ticket and was lucky to get one.

3. Avoid jet lag: James got a leaflet from his travel agent with some good advice on what to do and what to eat before you go on a long flight. It helps your body to adjust more quickly to a different time zone.

4. What to put into your briefcase: Put a clean shirt in a plastic bag, your neighbour might spill his coffee over your shirt during turbulence. A pair of ear-plugs come in handy when you need to concentrate on your documents or when you want to sleep.

Don'ts

1. Sleeping pills: Don't take them. You might be unable to react in an emergency.

2. Cellphones ("handies") and laptops: They both might present problems for the pilots since they interfere with the airplane's electronic devices. Moreover, it is considered bad manners to use portable phones in public.

3. Take a day off: Don't arrange an important meeting for the day of arrival after crossing several time zones – if you can avoid it. You will not be totally fit, even after a good flight. Visit your host country's consulate and collect information about how to do business there.

If you want more information see *Spotlight 10/96*

Chapter 1

B The hidden message

American speech	American thought
Now, I want you … to show those Europeans what made America great.	We are the most successful economic and democratic power. Our norms are the right ones.
The Europeans are our friends. So the Russians can't be Europeans.	Capitalists are friends. Europeans are capitalists. Russians are communists.
Europe – a bunch of states located off the east coast of the US.	Europe is so small compared to the USA. Is it really a continent?
Sell, sell, sell! And when you've conquered that market there's the Russians, the Arabs and the East.	Other nations think we are aggressive only because we are more efficient, dynamic and youthful.
Don't let flies breed on you.	Time is always money.

Hit them on the head

America – a country that has lept[1] from barbarism to decadence without touching civilisation.
John O'Hara

The thing that impresses[2] me most about America is the way parents obey[3] their children.
The Duke of Windsor

America is where you can become a blueblood[4] simply by having more greenbacks[5].
Bill Copeland

Nobody ever went broke[6] undererstimating[7] the taste of the American people.
Ross MacDonald

Losing is the great American sin. John Tunis, New York Times 1977

---

1 leap, lept, lept: springen 2 beeindrucken 3 gehorchen 4 Aristokrat 5 Dollar 6 Pleite machen 7 unterschätzen

FOCUS ON THE USA 1

(L) Going international: Last minute preparations

Do's

1. Talk with others who have lived in the country recently and learn from their experiences. Ask about differences between countries and peoples. This is the best remedy against culture shock.
2. Gather as much information as you can about the host country. Read about politics, art and religion on the plane. Visit your host country's consulate or national tourist offices for more information.
3. Study maps of the country and the city in order not to get lost.
4. Practise using the foreign currency in order not to get cheated by shop assistants, taxi drivers or waiters. You should feel comfortable when tipping waiters or porters.
5. Learn the measurement system so you can comfortably read signs, instructions and package descriptions.

Don'ts

1. Don't listen to friends who have had negative experiences in a foreign country. They might have been unable to adapt.
2. Don't make comparisons with how things are done at home. It will only increase your frustration.
3. Don't spend all the time in offices and hotels. Get out and make contacts.
4. Don't expect to be liked.

☺ Food for thought

Vice-president of a U.S. aluminium company: Before we invested in predeparture training[1], we had a very high return rate of people from Great Britain and the US involved in technology transfer in Venezuela. After we conducted[2] work-shops, the early failure attrition[3] dropped to zero ...

---

1 Training vor der Geschäftsreise 2 durchführen 3 Verschleiß

1 Chapter

(V) Vocabulary to help you with the text

a chip off the old block	wie der Vater so der Sohn
a rolling stone gathers no moss	wer rastet, der rostet
adjust	sich anpassen
affect	beeinträchtigen, beeinflussen
aid	Hilfe
avoid	vermeiden
be bred	aufwachsen
be aware of something	sich einer Sache bewußt sein
beneath	unter
bluntness	Direktheit, Grobheit
brash	ungestüm, aufdringlich
briefcase	Aktenkoffer
brusque	brüsk, barsch, schroff
buddy (AE)	Kumpel, Kamerad
cabbage	Kohl (hier: Dollars, Moneten)
chat	plaudern
collect information	Informationen sammeln
come in handy	gelegen kommen
comparison	Vergleich
consider	betrachten, halten für
don't let the flies breed on you	schlage keine Wurzeln
dude	Bursche, Kerl
ear plugs	Ohrstöpsel (Ohropax)
emergency	Notfall
federal state	Bundesstaat
frequent-flyer	Vielflieger
gather	sammeln
grains of truth	Körner der Wahrheit
greenback	Dollar
guess	meinen, raten
hacked from the same rock	aus dem gleichen Holz geschnitzt
host country	Gastland
hug	umarmen, drücken

FOCUS ON THE USA 1

inexperienced	unerfahren
insubordination	Ungehorsam
interfere with	stören
lack (v.) patience	keine Geduld haben
let's get to the point	kommen wir zur Sache
loot	Beute; hier: Kies, Knete
manners	Manieren, Benehmen
measurement	Maß, Maßeinheit
off the coast of America	vor der Küste von Amerika
prejudice	Vorurteil
pump someone's hand	jemandes Hand lange und kräftig schütteln
receive	erhalten
recently	kürzlich
remedy	(Heil-)Mittel
reputation	Ruf
sales call	Verkaufsgespräch
sample	Warenmuster
see ya!	bis dann, auf bald
self-confidence	Selbstvertrauen
slap someone on the shoulder	jemandem auf die Schulter hauen
subordinate	Untergebener
subtlety	Feinheit
successful	erfolgreich
unseemly	ungehörig
valuable	wertvoll

Chapter 1

B Our American crossword puzzle

Across: 1 the Statue of Liberty comes from this country, 7 ? from the same rock, 8 shake a hand violently, 10 a rolling stone ? no moss, 12 music is not Dave's ?, 14 English for 'Muster', 16 a typical American, 17 English for 'dudes', 18 opposite of 'receive' (a letter), 19 colloquial: money.

Down: 1 the US is a ? state, 2 another word for 'help', 3 he's a ? off the old block, 4 you do it on s.o.'s shoulder, 5 colloquial American for 'you', 6 short for 'United Kingdom', 7 Russian politicians do it, 9 which state is James from?, 11 music is not my cup of ?, 13 Dave pumped one, 14 don't pump a hand, ? it! , 15 rolling stones don't gather it,

Help: opposite: Gegenteil, colloquial: umgangssprachlich

FOCUS ON THE USA
Making friends the American way

Chapter 2

🙂 Time for a smile

On board of the plane to London, James Kelly was sitting between Mr Bossybitch from London and Mr MacGregor from Edinburgh. "And where are you from?" the Scot asked Jamie. "From God's own country," replied the American. "Hmm," said the Scotsman, "then you've got a very poor Scottish accent."

Chapter 2

First encounters on board an airplane

Mr Ron Bossybitch (**B**) and James Kelly (**J**) are sitting next to each other on board of a Delta flight 42356 from New York to London (by the way, both characters are real persons who the authors know only too well).

(Aircraft engines in the background)

B: Oh, I don't know if I feel well.

J: Now man, just breathe deeply. What's the problem? There are years of solid American technology supporting this pile of rusting metal.

B: What do you mean "rusting"?

J: Just a figure of speech. Now you just drink a bourbon and you'll feel fine. *(Slapping B. on the back in a somewhat overfriendly way – at least that's how Bossybitch saw it).*

B: *(coughing).* I say, I say. Hold on a bit. Not so hard!

J: Oh, I'm sorry man. I didn't realise you were so sick.
(To the air hostess) Stewardess, bring my buddy a double bourbon. That'll fix him up. By the way, call me Jamie, James Kelly from SASL, Sports Aids for the Slow Learner. We sell them in sixpacks.

B: How smart you Americans are! What's taking you to little, cold England, if I might ask?

J: Just doing a bit of little old business. Is there really any other reason for travelling so far away from the real world?

B: Well, I beg your pardon, but I sincerely hope there are other enticements in a visit to the oldest democracy in the world.

J: Such as what? ... Oh, yes, of course, shopping!

B: Well, I was rather thinking of culture, history, cuisine, the hospitality of the natives.

J: What the hell's cuisine? Some sort of police inquiry?

B: Certain classes in society would understand it as cooking.

J: Oh, you mean food. Right on! Food's important but I'm damn sure they've got some McDonald's joints in the UK.

B: I'm sure I wouldn't really know .

J: Don't worry. I'm certain they've got them there even if it's not the original burger.

B: I'm sure I couldn't care less.

J: Hey man, don't get all shook up! You can be sure there're other things I'm hooked on. *(Placing his hand upon B.'s knee).*

B: Excuse me, would you? *(Brushing James' hand away).*

FOCUS ON THE USA

Perhaps you could name me one, just by the way, as it were?
J: Sure I can. Look! Your Royal Family. They're the greatest! I bet you're all just waiting in line to get the top job. Do you know she's the richest woman in the world?
B: Well, personally I'm not very much in favour of all that sort of thing.
J: Course you are! Every Brit loves the Queen.
B: And I don't particularly like being called a Brit. I'm from Scotland.
J: Come on, man. The Royal Family is the greatest institution. They're so representative. Better than the president. And they don't pay a cent of tax.
B: Some people might say they don't do a day's work, either.
J: Could be, but in the States we know that you Brits are suffering from a lack of work ethic. You don't like to work. We call it the British disease.
B: I beg your pardon. That's a bit over the top. I'm not sure I can go on with this.
J: Don't worry! I'm half Irish myself. My grandfather is from Port Rush. Look! We're coming down now. There you go. You survived the flight. And if you ever happen to be in St Paul, just drop in for a drink. Here's my card. I'm sure we're going to be good friends. *(Slapping him on the shoulder).*
B: UghRR!

 Task 1: Train your brain

Do you understand what these lines really mean?

1. this pile of rusting metal
    a the aircraft
    b Bossybitch's old-fashioned laptop
    c the uncomfortable seats of the plane

2. travelling so far from the real world
    a travelling over the ocean
    b leaving the United States
    c travelling to Britain

3. a visit to the oldest democracy
    a a visit to Europe
    b a visit to Nottingham
    c a visit to Britain

Chapter 2

B Task 2: Understanding American English

Here are some American expressions from the dialogue and James' letter (page 29). Can you translate them into British English?

These words will help you: friend, devil, offended, I like, penny, outlet, completely right, New York, whisky

It's almost as big as the Big Apple. ....

Right on. ....

Don't get all shook up! ....

What the hell's cuisine? ....

There're things I'm hooked on. ....

They don't pay a cent of tax. ....

They've got some McDonald's joints. ....

A double bourbon for my buddy. ....

(For the solution see our key in the appendix)

M Mind your manners

What you should not say to a Scot.
- → I'm your Conservative candidate
- → Got any Irish whiskey?
- → Jimmy, where are your trousers?
- → What do you like about the English?
- → How about buying me a drink?
- → You would be nothing without your North-Sea oil.

☺ Time for a smile

An Englishman was boasting[1] that some of his ancestors[2] had been in the ark[3] with Noah. "At the time of the flood," retorted[4] the Scot, "we, the MacGregors, had our own boat."

---

1 prahlen 2 Ahnen 3 Arche 4 erwidern

FOCUS ON THE USA

Task 3: Did you get the hidden message?
Match figures against numbers

They say	They think
1. What's taking you to little cold England, if I might ask?	a These Europeans are so old-fashioned.
2. Excuse me, would you?	b Why don't you stay where you come from?
3. I hope there are other enticements in a visit to the oldest democracy?	c Keep your sticky fingers off my knickerbockers.
4. I must remember to turn my watch back five hundred years.	d You Yanks have no culture. You're only interested in money and shopping.

Task 4: American manners

"And if you ever happen to be in St. Paul, just drop in for a drink," said Jamie. Let's imagine for a moment that you accept such an invitation and – which is rather unlikely – that he still remembers your name.

Do you know what to say or to do? True or False   T F

1. If you are invited to an American home, you should bring flowers for the hostess.
2. Americans normally wish each other "Good appetite" before they begin a meal together.
3. It is considered polite to leave a little bit of food on your plate when you have finished eating.
4. Guests usually offer to help in the kitchen.
5. If you need to go to the toilet ask "May I use your toilet, please?"
6. When they ask you "How do you like the USA?" they expect you to give a frank and honest answer.
7. If you feel hot, don't ask if you can open a door or a window. Everything is air-conditioned.

Chapter 2

B Task 5: Patch work – Airport English
Phrases you and James might need when going on a flight.

unattended		check-in desk		baggage
	lounge		aisle seat	
proceed		book		boarding
	allowances		depart from	

Now it's your turn. Put the patches in the right places.

I'd like to .... an early flight from New York to London, please.

Where's the ...., please?

Could I have an ...., please?

Which gate do I .... ?

How many pieces of .... do you have?

Have you left your luggage .... at any time?

Excuse me, where is the departure .... ?

What are my duty-free .... ?

Flight number 492 to London is now .... at gate 25.

Would all passengers for flight number LH 432 please .... to gate 52 immediately.

☺ Time for a smile

If you can speak three languages you are trilingual[1].
If you can speak two languages you're bilingual[2].
If you can only speak one language – you're American.

1 dreisprachig 2 zweisprachig

FOCUS ON THE USA 2

L) Typical American: Letter to America

Dear Jane,
I miss you a lot. I've finally arrived in Europe. I'm in London. It's some sort of state capital. Quite a lot of people. Somebody told me about ten million but I can't believe that. It would mean it's almost as big as the Big Apple and I'm sure that's not possible. By the way, I met a nice English character on the plane. Not a good traveller. But he was very friendly. He was really interested in our American attitude to Europe. I invited him over to the real world. He seems to be interested in American food. He was surprised that I was so informed about their Royal Family. I even knew about the trouble with Lady Di. I guess he was somehow glad to talk about that.
They're a strange bunch, though. You don't know what they're trying to say. Well, I was thinking to myself on the plane, "I'm off to England. I must remember to turn my watch back five hundred years." Ha, ha, it's only a joke. Well, I've got my first meeting in England tomorrow in Nottingham, two hours north of London.
Think about me,

Yours Jamie.

  Task 6: The travelling manager's country quiz: Britain

There are some useful books for preparing for a business trip abroad. James Kelly is not what you would call a bookworm, so he has bought something light, with lots of jokes, crosswords and quizzes. Here is the quiz James was studying during his flight to the old world. James got most of the questions right. Isn't that a challenge? How many points will you score.

Part 1: People and Politics
1. How many countries does Great Britain consist of?
2. How many Parliaments are there in the United Kingdom?
3. In which part of the UK does religion play an important role in everyday life?

Chapter 2

4. How many per cent of the population claim to have no religion?
5. The UK has a population of about 57 million. How many live in England?
    - **a** 27 million
    - **b** 37 million
    - **c** 47 million
6. How many inhabitants has London got?
    - **a** 5 million
    - **b** 7 million
    - **c** 9 million
7. Who lives in the centre of London?
    - **a** the very rich
    - **b** the very poor
    - **c** the very rich and the very poor
8. Which is the British constitution?
    - **a** the Bill of Rights
    - **b** the Declaration of Independence
    - **c** the Magna Charta
    - **d** Britain hasn't got a written constitution.
9. The Parliament consists of two chambers
    - **a** the Senate and the House of Representatives
    - **b** Labour and Tories
    - **c** the House of Lords and the House of Commons
10. Which of the two chambers is more powerful?

Part 2: Bosses and workers
1. How many per cent of the working population are self-employed?
    - **a** 38%
    - **b** 24%
    - **c** 13%
2. Why do UK companies have greater freedom to hire and fire than in Germany?
3. How does the average British person prefer to work?
    - **a** on their own rather than share the responsibility with others; they are individualists
    - **b** in a team with which they can identify
    - **c** with people of their own class

FOCUS ON THE USA

4. In which country do companies spend the least money on training their staff?
    - a Germany
    - b France
    - c Britain
5. How many per cent of the work force in Britain are women?
    - a 45 %
    - b 34 %
    - c 18%
6. Women are more often found in managerial positions than in other European countries. Is that statement correct?
    - a Yes
    - b No
7. Why are 75% of new cars bought by companies?
    - a It allows a manager to avoid taxes on income.
    - b For many companies it is a matter of prestige to have a big fleet of cars.
    - c Company cars are changed more often than elsewhere.
8. How do you sign a business letter to a business partner whose name you know?
    - a yours faithfully
    - b yours truly
    - c yours sincerely
9. How do you sign a business letter to a business partner whose name you don't know?
    - a yours faithfully
    - b yours sincerely
    - c yours truly
10. What does it mean when a partner says to you, "Don't call us. We'll call you"?
    - a He is not interested in what you have to offer.
    - b He wants to be polite and save you the trouble of calling.
    - c He can't tell when he will be at the office.

2 Chapter

(V) Vocabulary to help you with the text

aircraft engines	Triebwerke
aisle seat	Sitz im Gang
attitude	Einstellung, Haltung
average	Durchschnitts-
book a flight	einen Flug buchen
breathe	atmen
bunch; a strange ~	ein sonderbarer Haufen
character	Person; Charakter
constitution	Verfassung
cuisine	Küche, Gastronomie
departure	Abreise, Abflug
disease	Krankheit
don't get all shook up	seien Sie nicht gleich beleidigt
encounters	Begegnungen
enticements	Anreize
Gaelic	gälisch (keltisch)
hospitality	Gastfreundschaft
hostess	Gastgeberin
I sincerely hope	ich hoffe aufrichtig, daß ...
I'm hooked on these things	ich bin scharf auf so was
inquiry	Befragung
joint	Rauschgift
managerial position	leitende Stellung
native	Eingeborener, Einheimischer
old-fashioned	altmodisch
pile	Haufen
proceed to	begeben Sie sich zu, nach
reward	Belohnung
squid (slang)	Pfundnote
survive	überleben
tax-free allowances	zollfreie Mengen
that'll fix him up	das richtet ihn wieder auf
that's a bit over the top	das geht etwas zu weit
trade-unions	Gewerkschaften

unattended   unbeaufsichtigt
wait in line   in der Schlange warten
work ethic   Arbeitsethik, -moral

☺ Hit them on the head

Silence[1] can be defined as conversation with an Englishman.
Heinrich Heine

When it's three o'clock in New York, it's still 1938 in London.
Betty Miller (1978)

If you want to eat well in England eat three breakfasts.
W. Somerset Maugham

It's good to have one foot in England; it is as good to have the other out of it.
Henry James

An Englishman is a creature who thinks he is being moral when he is only being uncomfortable[2].
George Bernard Shaw

I did a picture[3] in England one winter and it was so cold I almost got married.
Shelly Winters

In England rudeness[4] has a quite different technique. If someone on the Continent told you an obviously[5] untrue story, you would remark[6], "You are a liar, Sir, and a rather dirty one at that." In England you just say, "Oh, is that so?" or "That's rather an unusual story, isn't it?"
George Mikes

---

1 Schweigen   2 unbequem   3 Film   4 Grobheit   5 offensichtlich   6 bemerken

Chapter 2

B Our international crossword puzzle

Across: 1 it's the opposite of 'arrival', 6 middle part of a plane, 7 NY is called the Big ?, 8 please ? to gate 52, 13 meeting, 15 you do it with s.o.'s hand, 16 city in the USA known for cars, 18 don't forget to ? your flight, 19 waiting room at the airport

Down: 1 greenback is a ?, 2 big US telephone company, 3 my flight ? Paris is at 2 a.m. 4 ? stones don't gather moss, 5 English for 'Einheimische(r)', 8 a ? of rusting metal, 9 complete: Right ?, 10 don't smoke one, it's illegal, 11 American English for 'friend', 12 you are his guest, 14 where do I ? in, please?, 17 America is God's ? country.

Chapter 3

FOCUS ON BRITAIN
One language – two minds

😊 Time for a smile: How to be British

If you want to be really British, you must become a hypocrite[1]. How to be a hypocrite? An example explains things better than the best theory. I had a drink with an English friend in a pub when a German bomb exploded about a hundred yards away. I was honestly frightened[2], and when a few seconds later I looked around, I could not see my friend anywhere. At last I noticed that he was lying on the floor, flat as a pancake[3]. When he realized that nothing particular[4] had happened in the pub he got up a little embarrassed[5], flicked[6] the dust off his suit, turned to me with a superior[7] smile and said: "Good heavens! Were you so frightened that you couldn't move?"

Adapted from George Mikes, *How to be an Alien*

---

1 Heuchler 2 ehrlich erschrocken 3 Pfannkuchen 4 nichts Besonderes 5 verlegen
6 schnippen 7 überlegen

Chapter 3

🎧 Lunch at the Golf Club

James arrives at the Golf For Everyone and Country Club, the G.F.E.C.C., where he has an appointment with the director, Mr Johnson. Although it is rather warm, about 19°C., Jamie is wearing a Burberry raincoat which looks quite expensive.

James (J), Director Johnson (D), Charles, a waiter (C)

D: So, Mr Kelly, let's take that table in the corner. It's more private.

J: Great! Then we'll be away from the window and we won't have to look at your English weather. You're famous for it, you know.

D: Oh, is that so? Actually, I thought the weather was quite mild today. Still not as good as in the States, I suppose.

J: Oh, back home you can get any sort of weather you want. You just got to travel.

D: How interesting! Well, let's order, shall we? Here's the menu. What do you fancy as an apéritif? And what about an hors d'œuvre?

J: Well, I'm not sure I like hors d'œuvres. I've never eaten one as far as I know.

D: That's what we call the small things before the main course.

J: God man! You mean "starters". I'll have the shrimp salad then. Jesus, it's really great to be here. So much culture in England. So much history. There are so many old buildings around. Of course, back in the States we would have torn them all down and put up new modern structures by now.

D: You Americans are so clever. What do you fancy as a main course.

J: I'd like a good old T-bone steak like back home. You got anything like that?

D: Well, I'm sure we could rustle up a steak for you. Charles, could you take our order, please?

C: Certainly, sir.

J: My God, you guys are so formal. It's a real trip. Just grill me a steak. Can't go wrong with that, can you?

C: So that will be one sirloin steak grilled, sauté potatoes and vegetables.

J: Forget the sautés and vegetables. Just steak and French fries. Solid stuff.

C: Thank you, sir, and yourself, Mr Johnson?

D: I'll take the plaice, thank you, Charles.

C: Shall I bring a bottle of Bordeaux red, sir?
D: I think we'll take a half bottle of white and a half of red.
J: Gosh, no, I need a coke. That's the only thing I drink. Everything else is unhealthy.
C: Anything else, sir?
D: No, thank you, Charles, that's all for the moment. By the way, Charles, has the weather been like this all morning?
C: Yes sir, a very mild day today for a day in April, isn't it?
D: Yes indeed. I remember exactly the same sort of April day in 1967.
C: Yes, I remember too.
D: Or was it in 1976?
C: Yes, I think it was. Rain in the morning, a bit of sunshine and …
J: *(to himself)* So it's true what they say about the English.
(20 minutes later - clattering of plates)
C: Your steak, sir.
J: Jesus, I can't eat a steak without ketchup. Can you bring me the real stuff, American ketchup, please?
C: Certainly, sir, but will British be good enough?
J: Better than nothing. You know, Mr Johnson, it's almost like being back home here. It's so civilized. Wouldn't you like to live in the States for a while? To experience the hi-tech world?
D: Actually I've never thought about it.
J: Great, I'm really beginning to get the hang of this country. A few more days and I'll have it all under control.
D: Well, perhaps you will. I suggest we finish our lunch peacefully and then I'll show you our golf course and the facilities. There we can discuss your suggestions over a glass of, ehm, coke at the club house.
J: Sounds good.

☺ Time for a smile

The weather – this is the most important topic in the land… On the continent (or in the States), wanting to describe someone as exceptionally dull, you remark: "He is the type who would discuss the weather with you." In England … you must be good at doing just that.

George Mikes, *How to be an Alien*

3 Chapter

B Task 1: Train your brain

Let's see how good your short-term memory is.

1. Where does the meeting take place?
   - **a** at a golf club
   - **b** on the golf course
   - **c** at the facilities

2. What did James order as hors d'oeuvre?
   - **a** some starters
   - **b** a shrimp salad
   - **c** nothing

3. What does Mr Johnson eat?
   - **a** beef
   - **b** lamb
   - **c** fish

4. When and where are they going to talk business?
   - **a** at the club-house
   - **b** on the golf course
   - **c** at a restaurant

B Task 2: Understanding American English (1)

Look again at the text and find the American English phrases.

You've just got to travel.	....
Do you have anything similar?	....
Oh, my dear!	....
Thanks, no, I'd fancy a coke.	....
I'm beginning to understand this place.	....
It's fantastic.	....

B Task 3: Understanding American English (2)

James asked Charles to explain English food to him. Charles gave him two lists with English and American snacks to match them off.

American English	British English
1. French fries	a steak and lobster
2. cookie	b crisps
3. biscuit	c biscuit
4. surf-and-turf	d scone
5. potato chips	e chips

FOCUS ON BRITAIN 3

B Task 4: The hidden message (1)

The English often mean the opposite of what they say. Faint praise damns as surely as criticism. Let's read between the lines.

Can you match thought against speech?

Director Johnson says	Director Johnson thinks
1. You Americans are so clever.	a I would not dream of doing a thing like that.
2. Oh, is that so?	b Stupid foreigner!
3. Actually, I've never thought about it.	c What a silly thing to say!
4. ... will British ketchup be good enough?	d What a bore you are!
5. How interesting!	e You chauvinist Yankee!

B The hidden message (2)

Americans have a different way of speaking and thinking.

James says	Mr Johnson thinks
There are so many old buildings around. ... back in the States we would have torn them down and put up modern structures by now.	They think they are the biggest and the newest and the richest, and all the others are a bit slow and old-fashioned.
Jesus, I can't eat a steak without ketchup. Can you bring me the real stuff, American ketchup, please?	They've no interest in or knowledge of foreign cultures - a complete lack of curiosity.
Then we'll be away from the window and we won't have to look at your English weather.	Another impolite statement. They often say irritating and provocative things.
Oh, back home you can get any sort of weather you want.	Constant comparisons with how things are at home! We are not going to change for you.

Chapter 3

B Task 5: Patch work – At the restaurant

menu		take		booked
	corner		recommend	
for two		receipt		fancy
	what about		accept	

Put the patches in the right place:

A table .... , please.
Have you .... a table, sir?
Could we have that table in the .... ?
Waiter, could we have the ...., please?
What do you .... today?
Charles, could you .... our order, please?
What do you .... as an apéritif?
And .... an hors d'œuvre?
Could I have a .... , please?
Do you .... credit cards?

☺ Time for a smile

English views on other nations are very simple: they are all bloody foreigners. Swedish customs officials[1] at Arlanda airport were puzzled[2] by the behaviour of a gentleman who, long after all passengers had passed through immigration control, ran up and down with a bewildered[3] look on his face. Finally, one of the Swedes went up to him and asked why he had not come through passport control. "I don't know where my line[4] is," replied the gentleman. "There it says "Swedes" and here it says "Foreigners". But I am neither[5] a Swede nor[6] a foreigner. I'm an Englishman."

Richard D. Lewis, *When Cultures Collide*

---

1 Zollbeamte 2 verwundert 3 verwirrt 4 Durchgang 5 weder ... 6 noch

FOCUS ON BRITAIN 3

 Task 6: Watch their ways

"We have everything in common with America nowadays, except of course, the language," said the British author Oscar Wilde.

The American is frank and blunt. He exaggerates and loves the sensational.	The Englishman is more modest and diplomatic. He is known for his understatement.

Match American English (left) and British English.

1. Jack'll blow his top.
2. You're talking bullshit.
3. You gotta be kidding.
4. I tell you, I can walk away from this deal.
5. Bean-counters drive me mad.

a Accountants can be frustrating.
b How interesting, however ...
c I'm not quite with you on that.
d Our chairman might disagree.
e I'm afraid we all have to do our homework.

 Time for a smile

James was being driven around London by Mr Johnson. As they passed Buckingham Palace James asked: "Say, that's not a bad little joint[1]. How long did it take to put that up[2]?" "A couple of years, I suppose," said Mr Johnson. "Gosh!" said James. "We'd have thrown that up in six weeks back home."
Shortly afterwards they passed St. Paul's cathedral. "Gee, that's elegant. How long did that take to build?" Mr Johnson, becoming irritable[3], said "About three months."
"In America we'd have that up in a month," boasted[4] the American. Then they drove past the Houses of Parliament. "Jeepers, what a nice little hut. How long were they working on that?" Mr Johnson sniffed, stared out of the window and said, "Well, it wasn't there when I passed last night."

....

1 hier: Schuppen 2 bauen, aufstellen 3 gereizt 4 prahlen

Chapter 3

B Task 7 : Country quiz – British manners

1. Is it true what they say about the English?
   - **a** The English shake hands only in formal encounters.
   - **b** Businessmen don't shake hands.
   - **c** They shake hands. It all starts with a handshake.

2. James has an appointment with Mr Johnson, who is waiting for him in his office. What do you think is most likely to happen?
   - **a** Mr Johnson will stretch out his hand first.
   - **b** James takes the initiative.
   - **c** Shaking of hands is not appropriate in this situation.

3. How should James introduce himself?
Should he say?
   - **a** I'm Mr James Kelly.
   - **b** I'm James Kelly.
   - **c** I'm Mr Kelly.

4. Suppose you are introduced to a potential customer. He asks the famous question "How do you do?" What is your reaction?
   - **a** Fine, thank you.
   - **b** And how are you?
   - **c** How do you do?

5. A good business partner arrives. How do you greet him?
   - **a** How are you, Paul?
   - **b** How do you do?
   - **c** Hi, Paul.

6. A colleague greets you: "How are you, Bob?" How do you react?
   - **a** How do you do?
   - **b** Fine, thank you.
   - **c** How are you?
   - **d** Thank you, fine.

7. James Kelly visits a company in Edinburgh.
James wants to be polite and says: I love your beautiful English countryside. Why is Mr McGregor not amused?

FOCUS ON BRITAIN 3

(L) Letter from England

Dear Dave,

The trip is going to be more complicated than we thought. The weather here in London is awful. The first thing I had to do on my arrival was to buy a raincoat, the real thing. They are quite expensive so you won't see a Brit running around in a Burberry - only Germans or Americans. Mr Johnson took me to the golf club where we had lunch. When I saw his raincoat I decided to treat him.

What service you get here! The waiter looked like a lord, however, he seems to need some retraining. He got it all wrong. I ordered biscuits and Charles brought what they call a scone; I asked for potato chips and he brought me French fries and so on ... He seemed to be more into discussing the weather than serving the clients.

Mr Johnson is a nice guy but a bad talker. He's always so vague. You never know what he means. I suspect he's got some private problems and his psychiatrist hasn't allowed him to talk about it yet. I think I was able to persuade him to place a large order. Afterwards he took me for a ride around the town. .... I invited him to our place for a drink. Well, I've got to rush. I'm off to Ireland as you know.

Yours Jamie.

(L) A page from Mr Johnson's Diary

What a day - had to put up with a typical American - tunnel vision and at the end of tunnel there is the contract - the ideal consumer, bought a Burberry - behaved in the club as if he owned it - no sense of history or culture. I showed him the sights of the town - he was only interested in measurements and man hours - kept telling me that in the US they build everything bigger and faster - got very angry - a very pushy businessman - clever - wanted to walk away with an order of a thousand SASL - I ordered five - otherwise not a bad fellow - invited me and my family over to St. Paul.

Chapter 3

Going international: Britain in a nutshell

Don'ts

1. Don't call your Glasgow business partners English. You are not in England when you are doing business in Glasgow. They are Scots (Irish in Belfast and Welsh in Cardiff).
2. Don't try to bribe business partners.
3. Don't address partners by their first names. They are not Americans. Wait till they say: "Call me Dave".
4. Neither praise nor criticise the royal family. It's not your Queen!
5. Don't make comparisons with your country.
6. Avoid personal questions (many British find the Americans and also the Germans too pushy).
7. Don't ask them to change their habits (to drive on the right, like the rest of the world, for example).

Do's

1. Always be punctual for business meetings.
2. Shake hands when meeting. It is not necessary for a woman to shake hands.
3. Presentations and negotiations should be impersonal except with close friends.
4. Be conservative in gifts and entertainment. Avoid any impression of bribery.
5. Never rush to the bus, ticket office or shop counter. The British are a nation of queuers and probably the only time they complain vociferously is when someone jumps the queue.

Mind your manners

What you should not say to a British Person.

→ What do you like about the Americans?
→ Is your Japanese boss treating you well?
→ These French play rugby remarkably well.
→ Strikes and trade unions - we call it the British disease.
→ Is it true what they say about Prince Charles?

FOCUS ON BRITAIN 3

 Going international: Meetings the British way

1. The Staff meeting

In Britain the meeting is the most important and time-consuming management tool. It is considered as a part of the work and not as a necessary evil. Even unimportant decisions are discussed, voted and put into practice.

Only the most formal meetings are opened and closed on time. Discussions may be controversial. But it is the chairperson's concern to avoid clashes. Loyalty to the boss and the company is stronger than even fundamental disagreement.

It is considered fair play not to influence members beforehand in order bring about a decision with the help of a lobby. It is usual first to listen to the arguments of the others and then to support a suggestion.

2. International meetings

The English feel superior to the rest of the world. At international meetings British members often give the impression that they are arrogant and that they have little to learn from members of more successful nations. They view the Irish as being wildly eccentric, the Welsh as dishonest and the Scots as dour and mean, the French are insincere, the Germans easily-led bullies, the Italians hysterical, the Spanish lazy and the Russians gloomy. And since most conferences are held in English, they easily win the war of the words. This adds to the picture of the arrogant British.

Americans, Germans and Scandinavians like to come straight to the point. The English are different. The majority of meetings begin and end with small talk.

A staff meeting without some concrete result is regarded as a failure which does not hold true for international meetings. Even in the absence of disagreement British managers will rarely make a final decision at the first meeting. It is advisable to go for a long-term relationship - not for the quick deal. So don't push them to sign a contract; they don't like to be hurried. Suggest that a final decision should be taken at the next meeting. Bargaining is not the norm, but some concessions will satisfy the British negotiator's interest in economy.

3 Chapter

(V) Vocabulary to help you with the text

accountant	Buchhalter
avoid	vermeiden
bargaining	Feilschen, Handeln
be into something	scharf sein auf
bean-counters	Erbsenzähler
blunt	plump, direkt
bore (n; v)	Langweiler; langweilen
bribe (v; n)	bestechen; Bestechungsgeld
bullshit	Scheißdreck
bully	Schläger, Tyrann
comparison	Vergleich
complain	sich beschweren, beklagen
concern	Sorge, Angelegenheit
controversial	strittig
cookie	Keks
crisps	Chips
damn	verurteilen
delay (v; n)	verzögern; Verzögerung
disease	Krankheit
dishonest	unehrlich
dour	mürrisch, stur
entertainment	Bewirtung
exaggerate	übertreiben
expensive	teuer
facilities	Anlagen, Einrichtungen
famous	berühmt
fancy	mögen
French fries	Pommes frites
get the hang of	kapieren
gift	Geschenk
habit	Gewohnheit
irritating	ärgerlich, lästig
jump the queue	sich vordrängen
lack patience	keine Geduld haben
menu	Speisekarte

FOCUS ON BRITAIN 3

modest	bescheiden
negotiator	Verhandlungspartner
opposite	Gegenteil
plaice	Scholle
praise	loben
pushy	aufdringlich, drängelnd
put into practice	etwas in die Praxis umsetzen
queue	Warteschlange
receipt	Quittung
recommend	empfehlen
rustle up	auftreiben
scone	Teegebäck
sirloin steak	Lendensteak
sound; that ~s good	gut klingen
starters	Vorspeisen
structures	Gebäude
suggest	vorschlagen
support a suggestion	einen Vorschlag unterstützen
suppose; I ~	ich nehme an, ich vermute
take something at face value	etwas für bare Münze nehmen
tear down (torn, torn)	abreißen
tool	Instrument, Werkzeug
vociferously	lautstark, schreiend

3 Chapter

B Our English crossword puzzle to test your memory

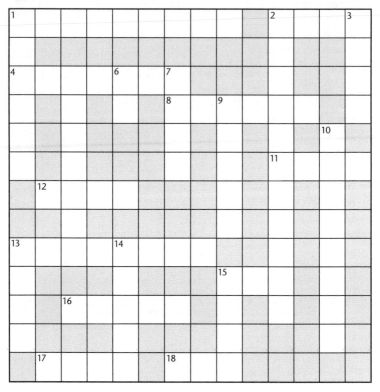

Across: 1 English for 'Handy', 2 Jamie got the ? of the country,
4 the publisher of this book, 8 'Do you ? credit cards?', 11 meetings are a management ?, 12 list of starters and dishes, 13 one of the authors of this book, 15 to ? the hang of something, 16 where do the Welsh live?, 17 what is 'plaice'?, 18 to ? something into practice

Down: 1 they wanted a table in the ?, 2 quality of good hosts, 3 'Please proceed to ? B 12', 5 the wife of your host, 6 he got the hang ? the country, 7 'Can I ? your orders, sir?', 9 English for French fries, 10 'The flight to London is now ?', 13 support (a suggestion), 14 inhabitant of Wales, 15 you offer it to your host

Chapter 4

FOCUS ON BRITAIN
Golf clubs for the temperamental player

🙂 Time for a smile

An Englishman and an American were shipwrecked on an island in the Pacific. The natives were very friendly and after six months the American was running a light railway, while the Englishman was still waiting to be introduced.

Chapter 4

Golf clubs for the temperamental player

> In the golf-course club-house (Pop plus sound of pouring brandy):
> James (**J**), Director (**C**), Johnson (**D**)

D: Are you sure you won't try a drop of this excellent brandy? It's fifteen years old. They stored it for fifteen years in oaken barrels. It's called Don Mendosa.

J: I don't like that old stuff. A good coke is all a man needs. It really peps me up.

D: Fine! Well, I believe business should be discussed in a relaxed atmosphere with a good cognac. Partners find a way, they muddle through but it seems to work.

J: Back home we don't like that sort of hit and miss tactic. Everything should be carefully worked out. Discipline. That's the ticket!

D: Well, if you think so. Ah, George could you bring me a Mendosa and a coca cola for the young man? Now, sir, down to business. What have you got that might interest me?

J: Listen, call me James. I'm sure we're going to hit it off.

D: Collin.

J: OK, Coll. Interest you? It'll knock your socks off! Check this out! Everyone who plays golf meets a guy who flies into a fit of rage every time he doesn't something quite perfectly.

D: Well, most of my partners have themselves under control ... relatively speaking.

J: That's because you're all aces at the sport. But what about the rest? *(knocking a fork against his coke glass).* Where the hell is the waiter? Hey, waiter, another coke! Now let's say your partner, he wants to let off steam. He's disappointed himself. He takes his club and smashes it against the nearest object. Wham, bam, thank you, ma'am.

D: I beg your pardon?

J: I mean, he's destroyed his golf club. Think about it! A potential customer comes to your club. He borrows your expensive clubs and destroys half of them. You can hardly prosecute him. But the bottom line is you've got the bill.

D: Well, first of all I'd like to point out that in our club people don't normally break equipment when they're losing a game.

J: Come on, man. Think of tennis. McEnroe did it all the time and he was a champion.

D: And, if I might add, he was an American. We're not the Wild West here, you know.

J: No, but for us you're not far from it with your lack of technology. Think of your savings.

D: Of course, at the end of the day we are a business in the end and we are obliged to consider the financial implications of everything we do but we're a club as well, and ...

J: Well, now you've got it! You're a business and you're the CEO. The profit's yours but so's the responsibility.

D: Yes, well, could you show me an example of the equipment?

J: You bet I can and you'll be blown away. I'll just open up this little box of goodies. It's on a daylight projector. And I've got some slides. *(Clanking of machinery)*. There! How does that grab you?

UNITED STATES PATENT OFFICE
3,087,728. Patented Apr.30, 1963
Breakable Simulated Golf Club
Ashly Pond III, Taos, N.Mex.
Filed Nov. 25, 1960. Serial No. 71,689.

This invention is a new and novel golf club. As in any field of competition, the urge to win causes an emotional drive which reaches an intense peak when, through inadvertence, poor judgement, or error in play, a mistake is made which causes the competitor to lose control of his temper.

pin

It is, therefore, one of the primary objects of this invention to provide a golf club which is conventional in appearance, and

---

pin: Stift

Chapter 4

>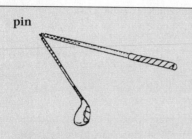
> pin
>
> which is deliberately constructed to break when used by a golfer in a fit of temper. Another object of this invention is to provide a golf club for temperamental golfers wherein the shaft of the club is deliberately constructed to break when struck against the ground, a tree, or other inanimate elements when the anger of the golfer reaches a mercurial height, and wherein the emotion of the golfer requires some physical manifestation to achieve emotional release.

J: Well, can't you see the money your member could save? After breaking a club all he has to do is to replace this pin.
D: Is that all there is to it?
J: Sure, that's the beauty. KISS: Keep it simple, stupid.
D: I quite like that little device, however I'm not sure that this type of instrument is of use to my members. They're hardly violent, you know.
J: There's aggression building up in all of us.
D: Yes, I see your point. If that's all, Mr Kelly, I have another appointment.
J: Right! I'll call you later for another date so that we can discuss prices. I'm sure we can do something special for you.
D: Perhaps. Anyway good-bye, and don't call us, we'll call you.
J: Why, thank you very much, Coll. See you later then.

☺ Time for a smile

Tina's golf trainer was impressed[1]. With her new 'breakable golf club', Tina gave the ball a mighty sweep[2] and got a hole in one stroke[3]. At the second tee[4] she swipes again. The ball lands on the green, rolls towards the hole and plops in. Tina turned to her trainer white and trembling[5]. "What's the problem, Tina?" asked the trainer. "You're the born golfer." "Christ, I thought I'd missed[6] that one," Tina sighed[7].

---
1 beeindruckt 2 Schwung 3 Schlag 4 Abschlag 5 zitternd 6 verfehlen 7 seufzen

FOCUS ON BRITAIN 4

B) Task 1: Train your brain

More than one answer might be correct.

1. What does Director Johnson think of James' product?
   - a He is interested. The breakable club would save money.
   - b He will call him back later and tell him his decision.
   - c He is not interested because British players are not violent.
2. What is the advantage of the Breakable Simulated Golf Club?
   - a It prevents the angry golfer from breaking his club.
   - b It helps the beginner to avoid mistakes.
   - c It doesn't break when the beginner makes a mistake.
3. What do you think? Is the breakable club a real US patent?
   - a It must be a joke, an invention of Bosewitz and Kleinschroth.
   - b I think it is an existing patent.

L) Letter from England

Hi Dave,

Well, this old Europe's real terrific. They're all so formal with waiters saying 'sir' and bowing to me. They've all got these weird accents, too. Like something from the 19th century. In my opinion they tend to use alcohol too much. People keep offering me cognac and wine. Can't do business with a light head!

Yesterday I had a business lunch with Coll from G.F.E., Golf For Everyone. I think SASL will score a big hit there. He seemed very interested and he's going to contact me.

In the evening I tried to play racket ball to keep in shape. I couldn't find a court so I played an old English game, squash. Perhaps we should check that market out, too.

Best regards
Jamie

☺ Time for a smile

James was invited by Collin Johnson. The host and his wife were playing a delicate duo on their grand piano. He listened for a while and then said, "That's nice. Very nice. But back home, me and my baby, we have a piano each."

Chapter 4

B Task 2: Understanding the Americans (1)

Match the numbers against the right letters.

1. The bottom line is ...
2. goodies
3. You're the CEO.
4. How does that grab you?
5. Sure!
6. You'll be blown away.
7. Check this out!

a Have a look at this!
b You'll be surprised.
c What do you think of that?
d You are the managing director.
e Of course!
f The final result is ...
g interesting, fine products

B Task 3: Watch their ways

Now that you have read about the language of businessmen you can match James' speech against the stereotypes?

What James says and ...	... why he says it
1. I'll call you later so that we can discuss prices.	a Americans are impatient, time is money.
2. OK, Coll. Interest you?	b The American way of life is best.
3. Where the hell is the waiter?	c Americans want to make the profit now.
4. It'll knock your socks off.	d They use violent language.
5. You're all aces at the sport.	e They get on first-name terms quickly.
6. I don't like that old stuff. A good coke is all a man needs.	f Americans are generous with compliments.

Typical American: The language of businessmen

The American language of business still reflects the life styles of the early settlers who domesticated the untouched wilderness and the adventurers who made a rush to the goldfields of Klondyke. They had no time for originality and elegance of speech. This is how Willy Lowman, the anti-hero in Arthur Miller's *Death of a Salesman* describes a successful business trip to his sons: "Knocked 'em cold in Providence, slaughtered 'em in Boston." Managers do not open markets, they conquer them like the pioneers who conquered the wilderness. Violent speech, tough talk and exaggerations still characterise the way many Americans speak. "It'll knock your socks off," says James or "Wham, bam, thank you ma'am" where the English would simply say "... and there you are".

That explains also why American businessmen drive a hard bargain. They are said to be the toughest in the world. On the other hand, they are easy to deal with because their business philosophy is uncomplicated. "KISS" is James Kelly's slogan, "Keep it simple and stupid." Making money as quickly as possible by hard work, speed and opportunism just like Willy Lowman's brother Ben who explains his business philosophy to his nephews: "Why, boys, when I was seventeen I walked into the jungle, and when I was twenty-one I walked out. And by God, I was rich."

James Kelly is the average American businessman: tough, aggressive impatient and dynamic, "Come on man ... think of your savings." He knows that he has to make money in order to be somebody in America, otherwise he is a nobody. If he calculates that he has 40 years to make four million dollars, then he has to make $ 100,000 per annum, $50 an hour, $400 a day and that 250 days a year. Time is money for James and his colleagues. They are less interested in a long-term business relationship. They want to make the profit now and that is why their speech is quick, aggressive and opportunistic.

Time for a smile

James Kelly, after a visit in Soho, London: "The American West is a place where men are men, but in Soho you can never be sure."

Chapter 4

B Task 4: Understanding the Americans (2)

Do you remember what James said?

British English	American English
I don't drink that kind of alcohol.	....
I'm certain we'll get on well.	....
... and there you are!	....
Try harder!	....
That's the great advantage.	....

L Typical British: The English businessman's language

While the American businessman is straightforward, says what he thinks and tends to make on-the-spot decisions, his British colleague is a good listener and keeps back his position as long as possible. He has hundreds of years of experience with India, the Middle and Far East. ("Well," said Collin Johnson, "I believe business should be discussed in a relaxed atmosphere with a good cognac.")

He rarely disagrees openly with your proposals. Just Like Mr Johnson he might say, "I quite like that little device" only to go on with, "however I'm not sure that this type of instrument is of use to my members." Vagueness and indirectness is one characteristic of his speech. He uses positive adjectives instead of negative ones, questions instead of statements; he adds words like "little, might, would quite, rather, slight, I'm afraid that ... " to soften his positions. This is part of what we call the typical English understatement. Here are a few examples:

He doesn't say	He says
Can I say a few words about ...	If I just might say a few words about ...
It is better to ...	Wouldn't it be better if ...

FOCUS ON BRITAIN 4

B Task 5: Say it the English way

Here are a few words to soften the statements: very positive / would/ quite / little/ not quite right / might / little / slight / some / a bit / not

He doesn't say	He says
That is impossible.	I'm afraid, that .... not be possible.
I like that device.	I .... like this .... device.
That's a negative attitude.	That's .... a .... attitude.
I think these figures are wrong.	I beg your pardon, but I'm afraid these figures are ....
We need more money for the project.	I'm afraid we .... need a .... more the money for the project.
We have a cash-flow problem.	I'm afraid we have a .... cash-flow problem.
I have reservations as to this project.	I have .... reservations as to the success of this project.
I think that is dangerous.	I'm afraid that might be .... dangerous.

☺ Hit them on the head

The American language is in a state of flux based on the survival of the unfittest.

                          Cyril Connolly, *The Sunday Times, 1996*

Typical American: "They don't stand on ceremony ... They make no distinction about a man's background, his parentage, his education. They say what they mean, and there is a vivid muscularity about the way they say it ... They are always the first to put their hands in their pockets. They press you to visit them in their own home the moment they meet you, and they are irrepressibly good-humoured, ambitious and brimming with self-confidence in any company. Apart from that I've got nothing against them."

                          Tom Stoppard, *Dirty Linen, 1976*

Chapter 4

V Vocabulary to help you with the text

achieve emotional release	Gefühle abreagieren können
add	hinzufügen
aggression builds up	Aggressionen stauen sich auf
appointment	Termin, Verabredung
average American	Durchschnittsamerikaner
be obliged to consider something	etwas überdenken müssen
bill	Rechnung
bottom line; and the ~ is	und das Resultat ist ...
box of goodies	Schachtel mit "Bonbons"
brim with self-confidence	vor Selbstbewußtsein überschäumen
cause an emotional drive	emotionalen Drang auslösen
drive	Schwung, Energie, Elan
CEO (Chief Executive Officer)	Direktor
check this out!	passen Sie mal auf!
conquer	erobern
conventional in appearance	normal aussehend
deliberately constructed to break	bewußt so konstruiert, daß er abknicken muß
destroy	zerstören
device	Gerät
exaggeration	Übertreibung
financial implications	finanzielle Auswirkungen
flux	Fluß
fly into a fit of rage	Wutanfall bekommen
grey matter	graue Zellen (Gehirn)
how does that grab you?	wie gefällt Ihnen das?
inadvertence	Unachtsamkeit
inanimate elements	nicht lebende Dinge
intense peak	hoher Grad, Spitzenwert
irrepressibly	unverwüstlich, nicht unterzukriegen
knighthood	Adelstitel
let off steam	Dampf ablassen
lose control of one's temper	die Kontrolle über sich verlieren

FOCUS ON BRITAIN 4

make no distinction	keinen Unterschied machen
muddle through	sich durchwursteln
muscularity	Muskelkraft, Stärke
oaken barrel	Eichenfaß
parentage	Abstammung
primary object	vorrangiges Ziel
prosecute	verklagen
racket ball	amerikanische Sportart, ähnlich wie Squash
reflect	widerspiegeln
relatively speaking	hier: mehr oder weniger
replace the pin	Stift ersetzen
reservations	hier: Vorbehalte
responsibility	Verantwortung
shaft of the club	Stiel des Golfschlägers
soften	mildern, abschwächen
straightforward	offen, direkt, unkompliziert
strike (struck, struck) against	schlagen gegen
temperamental	reizbar, leicht erregbar
the anger of the golfer reaches mercurial heights	der Golfspieler bekommt einen Jähzornsanfall
tough talk	robuste Sprache
urge to win	Trieb zu gewinnen
violent	heftig, gewalttätig
weird	verrückt, schrullig, sonderbar
wham, bam, thank you, ma'am	hier: und da haben Sie den Salat (urspr. sexueller Bezug)

Chapter 4

B A crossword puzzle to test your memory

Across: 1 English for 'Quittung', 5 American English for 'petrol', 7 part of London, 9 the opposite of 'mind', 11 'break' (a golf club), 12 complete: let steam ?, 14 part of the breakable golf club, 16 energy, urge, motivation, 17 English for 'hinzufügen', 19 It will knock your ? off, 22 Brandy matures in an ? barrel

Down: 2 American English for director, 3 nervous, easy to offend, 4 don't fly into a ? of anger, 5 the brain is called the grey ?, 6 repair the word: *fontes,* 7 part of the golf club, 8 they ? it off well together, 10 we're just muddling ?, 13 another word for 'hit' sth., 14 opposite of 'criticise', 15 keep it simple, stupid, 18 English for 'Verspätung', 20 to get ? well with someone, 21 calm down, ? some steam off

FOCUS ON IRELAND
Balls with a beep

Chapter 5

🙂 Time for a smile

Bridget O'Leary was trying to cash a cheque[1] in a Dublin bank. "Can you identify yourself, madam?" asked the clerk. "Certainly," said Bridget, reached into her handbag, took out a little mirror[2], looked in it and declared confidently[3], "Yes, it's me all right. I'd recognise[4] me anywhere."

---

1 Scheck einlösen 2 Spiegel 3 zuversichtlich 4 sich wiedererkennen

5 Chapter

Balls with a beep

James, on his whistle-stop tour of Europe, arrives in Belfast. The flight was not particularly comfortable and the food was cold. He takes a train to Galway and then a taxi to the Galway Golf Training Centre. Here he has an appointment with Mr O'Leary, the manager, at 7 p.m.

In the club-house – talking business. James (**J**), Mr O'Leary (**O**)

O: *(clinking of glasses)* So, let's raise our glasses to our good health. Cheers!

J: Oh, good health. Well, I really admit that this tastes better after the third or fourth glass.

O: Mr Kelly, can I ... ?

J: Just call me Jamie. I guess here you're not as formal as those English I've been visiting.

O: Fine then, Jamie, call me Sean. Let's come straight to the point! If you've got something of good quality that we can use and that can stimulate our business, we're interested. So let's hear it.

J: You bet your booties. I've got two or three little superstars here that'll blow your mind.

O: Let's take it step by step. No big surprises! Just give me an overview, no details at this stage.

J: Right on! From the macro to the micro. Well, we can offer you some instruments to support your golf learners. What percentage of first-timers or learners do you have here? Thirty, fourty percent?

O: No, actually it's sixty percent. You see we have a large seasonal tourist trade. Of course, we have our regulars ....

J: ... who are skilled enough already. Yes, but this large number of beginners. That's where we can help. Look at this chart. What do you see?

O: George, two more Guinness. Jamie, can I offer you some oysters with your Guinness?

J: Wow! Well, I don't actually eat fish ....

O: Now my lad, oysters are not fish. And you should know that Guinness and oysters are almost a national dish here in Ireland.

J: You don't say! I was sure Irish stew was the national dish.

O: That's a wonderful meal too, but it's more for the workforce. More sophisticated people appreciate Guinness and oysters.
J: Well, you can bet that I'll appreciate it, too. I'll certainly have a portion. Do you eat it with ketchup?
O: Catch up with what? Oh yes, your dynamite.
J: Oh, right, straight to the punchline. Fine! What do your beginners do when they get on that course for the first time?
O: They normally tee off, probably a bit short.
J: Right but is that all?
O: Most of them go straight into the rough.
J: Right on! That's where it's at.
O: I beg your pardon. Where what's at?
J: They're in the rough. They've lost the ball. They're angry, frustrated. And that's where SASL comes in.
O: I'm sure I've no idea what you're getting at.
J: Look at this chart! We've developed a golf-ball with a beeper in it. All the dimensions and the weight of the ball are the same as the standard ball.
O: George, two Jamesons, please. How do you activate the beep?
J: Idiot-proof. You have an actuator in the handle of your golf-club. What do you think now?
O: Well, blow me away!

B Task 1: Train your brain

How many golf learners does O'Leary have?
What are James and O'Leary eating and drinking?
What SASL product does James show to O'Leary?
How does it help the learner?

☺ Time for a smile

What's Dublin? Can you play it?
        Louis Armstrong

The Irish tug-of-war[1] team was disqualified for pushing[2].

---

1 Tauziehen 2 schieben, stoßen

5 Chapter

B Task 2: Patch Work – Small talk and business talk

offer		getting at		overview
	step by step		really admit	
raise		comes		national dish
	to the point		appreciate	

Now it's your turn. Put the patches in the right places.

So, let's .... our glasses to our good health.

I .... that this tastes better after the third or fourth glass.

Can I .... you some oysters with your Guinness?

Guinness and oysters are almost a .... here in Ireland.

I'll certainly .... it, too.

Let's come straight ....

And that's where SASL .... in.

I'm sure I've no idea what you're ....

Let's take it ....

Just give me an ...., no details at this stage.

M Mind your manners

What you should not say to an Irish person.
- → Does the priest know you're doing this?
- → You should try our Dallas Guinness.
- → Can you tell me how to get to ... ?
- → I never tell Irish jokes. Do you know this one? There were these two Chinamen, Paddy and Mick ... .

FOCUS ON IRELAND 5

 Task 3: Understanding American English

Can you match British and American English? Here is some help:
Gehweg, Kofferraum, Erdgeschoß, Ferngespräch.

American English	British English
1. sidewalk	a motorway
2. first floor	b long distance call
3. trunk	c boot
4. trunk call	d ground floor
5. freeway	e pavement

 Letter from Ireland

Dear Jane,

Yesterday was a day I'd almost rather forget. I was in Ireland. Well, I know my forefathers are Irish, but I'm not surprised they're having a problem to get up to date in this fast world. They seem to spend most of the time getting drunk on Guinness and whisky. And so did I. It went so quick. One minute I was okay, the next I seemed to be talking nonsense. (But so was Sean). That's the CEO, Mr O'Leary. He's okay, but I guess I blew it all there. Guess he didn't take me seriously.

Life is really slow over here. It's like it must have been back home five hundred years ago. What I notice here and back in Britain for that matter is that there's no service. You order a coffee and sure enough you get a good cup. But then that's it. They don't bring any more. If you want another you have to get the waitress' attention. And can you believe you have to pay again!!

Another crazy thing here in Europe. Each country is so small and so close. But it's a real hassle with the money. There's different money in each country. The exchange rate's a real rip-off.

See you
Jamie,

PS. Tomorrow I'm off to Frankfurt, Germany.

Chapter 5

Going international: A good place for investment

A well-trained workforce

How do the English see the Irish? They are for them what the East-Friesians are for the Germans, or the Belgians for the French: slow in their movements and slow on the uptake. However, research funded by the British government has found out that Irish-born inhabitants in Britain are twice as likely to hold university degrees as the true Brits. Maybe that is one reason why the government has passed a law that makes the publication of Irish jokes illegal.

Ireland is a good place for foreign investors. The workforce is by overall European standards young, well-educated, mobile and professional. The 900 foreign-owned companies already control 50 percent of the total turnover of the country. They employ 40 percent of the non-agricultural workforce. With 62 percent of the population in favour of the European Community (only 17 percent are against it) it is the most pro-European country compared to 28 percent in Britain, which is the least European country.

Ireland is a lousy market for cars. The Japanese have got the lionshare of 40 percent anyway. The Irish spend most of their money on food and drink. They are second in Europe regarding the consumption of butter, on the other hand they eat little cheese and buy few clothes.

The management

"The Irish managers," writes Paul Gibbs[1] "are among the shrewdest and most intelligent businessmen you will ever meet." They have a more flexible approach to organisation than the English. They give more importance to personal relationships, they have a talent for improvisation and a dislike of rigid systems and bureaucracy. Since they like doing business in a relaxed atmosphere meetings last longer than planned and they are less formal than in mainland Britain. Most managers are friends, former schoolmates or relatives. Often they are on first-name-terms with foreigners during the first meeting. The Irish like a good dinner, a good drink and a good conversation. However, since the law has been changed, your Irish host can no longer deduct a business dinner from the taxes. So be prepared that you might have to pay for your own lunch.

FOCUS ON IRELAND 5

Hosts and hospitality

At lunch time the Irish no longer drink as much alcohol as they used to do. A drink and a bottle of wine is all you can hope for. This will be different at dinner. You'd better make sure that your hotel is not too far from where your business partner lives. When he invites you to a pub, be prepared for your dinner and your conversation to be interrupted by saying hello to your host's friends, colleagues, the priest or his neighbours. That is part of the Irish way of life.

Sean O'Leary has invited James to his home. This is a sign that he has accepted our impossible Yankee to a certain degree. Now what present should James offer to his host and hostess? Flowers and chocolates, of course. Mr O'Leary would appreciate a bottle of brandy, whiskey or wine, because in Ireland there is a very high tax on all spirits.

Avoid subjects like religion or politics if you are not asked for your opinion. Be careful what you say about his competitor, he might be your host's uncle or cousin. Women in business, especially in high positions, is not a favourite subject either. The Irish and the Belgians share the greatest antipathy in the European Community towards working women.

For more we recommend: Paul Gibbs, *Euromanagement*.

☺ Time for a smile: The wit of the Irish

"I cannot understand," said Bridget, "why the milk company is complaining about a shortage of glass milk bottles. I've got thousands of them at home."

"What would you do if you found a million pounds, Mike?" asked Bridget. "Well, it all depends[1]," said Mike, "who had lost it. If it was a poor person I would certainly return it."

Mike was leading the evening prayers in his household:
"Let us now pray for the people in uninhabited[2] areas of the world."

---

1 es kommt darauf an 2 unbewohnt

5 Chapter

B Task 4 : The travelling manager's Irish country quiz

1. The capital of Northern Ireland is
- **a** Dublin
- **b** Belfast
- **c** Cork

2. The capital of the Republic of Ireland is
- **a** Dublin
- **b** Limerick
- **c** Galway

3. How many people in Ireland speak German? Have a guess.
- **a** 8%
- **b** 4%
- **c** 2%

4. How many people live in the Republic of Ireland?
- **a** 4 million
- **b** 7 million
- **c** 11 million

5. In Ireland you have to drive
- **a** in the middle
- **b** on the right
- **c** on the left

6. Who is the greatest investor in Ireland?
- **a** Great Britain
- **b** the USA
- **c** Germany

7. With Irish business partners you are quickly on first-name terms.
- **a** true
- **b** false
- **c** neither

8. What is a typical Irish dish apart from Irish stew?

FOCUS ON IRELAND 5

9. What is Murphy's?
- **a** the logic of Murphy's laws 'Why Things Go Wrong'
- **b** a famous Irish whisky
- **c** a well-known porter brewed in Limerick

10. Who is the patron saint of Ireland?
- **a** St. Patrick
- **b** St. George
- **c** St Bonifaz

11. What second language is spoken in Ireland?
- **a** Celtic
- **b** Gaelic
- **c** Iric

12. What could you not advertise in the media?
- **a** medicine
- **b** tobacco
- **c** spirits (alcohol)

(V) Vocabulary to help you with the text

activate	auslösen
actuator	Auslöser
admit	zugeben
antipathy	Abneigung
appreciate	mögen, schätzen
approach; the ~ to do something	die Art, etwas anzupacken
at this stage	zu diesem Zeitpunkt
beeper	Piepser
bet one's bottom dollar	seinen letzten Pfennig wetten
compare	vergleichen
competitor	Rivale, Konkurrent

Chapter 5

contradiction	Widerspruch
deduct from the taxes	von den Steuern absetzen
dislike of rigid systems	Abneigung gegen starre Systeme
favourite subject	Lieblingsthema
from the macro to the micro	vom Allgemeinen zum Besonderen
fund	finanzieren
good health	auf Ihre Gesundheit
hassle; no ~ (AE)	kein Problem
hostess	Gastgeberin
improve	verbessern
mainland	Festland
overview	Überblick
oysters	Austern
pass a law	ein Gesetz verabschieden
patron saint	Schutzheiliger
rank	Rang, Stellung
raise something	etwas heben, erhöhen
regulars	Stammkunden
research	Forschung, Untersuchung
rip-off	Wucher
schoolmate	Schulkamerad
shrewd	scharfsinnig, gescheit
skilled	geschickt, geübt
slow on the uptake	schwer von Begriff
sophisticated	kultiviert, raffiniert, hochstehend
starter	Vorspeise
stimulate business	das Geschäft beleben
straight into the rough	direkt ins Gebüsch
support	unterstützen
taste	schmecken, kosten
tee off (v.)	abschlagen (beim Golf)
that's where it's at	das ist der springende Punkt
turnover	Umsatz
university degrees	akademische Abschlüsse
vitally important	lebenswichtig, sehr wichtig
weight	Gewicht
whistle-stop tour	Reise von Ort zu Ort

FOCUS ON IRELAND 5

☺ Hit them on the head: from James Kelly's Irish diary

O'Leary offered me Guiness and oysters. Well, as Woody Allen said: I prefer my food dead – not sick[1], not wounded – dead.

I did not say the steak was tough[2]. I just wanted to say that I haven't seen the mule[3] that used to stand outside the golf-club for a long time.

Afterwards we had Irish coffee. In a single glass we got everything that is unhealthy: alcohol, caffeine, sugar and fat.

And then there was that Irishman who got stranded for an hour in a supermarket when the escalator[4] broke down[5].

---

1 krank 2 zäh 3 Esel 4 Rolltreppe 5 eine Panne haben

5 Chapter

B Our Irish crossword puzzle

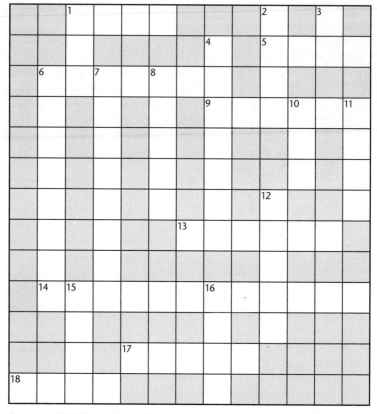

Across: 1 British English for 'trunk', 5 straight ? the rough, 6 American English for 'hors d'oeuvre', 9 the Irish eat it with Guinness, 13 German for 'turnover', 14 co-author of this book, 17 they keep your feet warm, 18 sound James' balls make

Down: 1 you ? your bottom dollar, 2 keep it simple, stupid, 3 that's where it's ?, 4 British English for 'hassle', 6 American English for 'pavement', 7 repair the word: acavitet, 8 British English for 'boot', 10 blow one's ?, 11 position of an employee, 12 from ? to micro, 15 love, appreciate, 16 James' favorite drink

Chapter 6

FOCUS ON GERMANY
Filling in forms in Frankfurt

☺ Time to smile at the Germans

The typical German tourist:
As soon as he gets to Paradise he will ask for picture postcards.

And there was this good-looking East-Friesian who went surf-riding. His horse drowned[1].

They have passed a law[2] to make attendance at the German Bundestag obligatory – by twelve votes to four.

---

1 ertrinken 2 ein Gesetz verabschieden

Chapter 6

Filling in forms in Frankfurt

At Frankfurt Airport James Kelly walks through customs and immediately gets lost in a horde of information signs.

James (**J**), Passer-bye (**P**), Lady (**L**), Clerk (**C**)
* = typical German mistakes

J: Jesus, I can't make any of this out. All these arrows and letters. It's not logical. I'll just check it out with this guy. Excuse me, sir, could I have a moment of your time?

P: Wie bitte? Sorry, I'm in a hurry, my flight ... wurde aufgerufen. There's the plan of the airport, over there. It explains the system.

J: But sir, I've got myself lost here.

P: Just ask at the info. There you *become a plan. It's simple, systematic and logical. Tschüs.

J: Jesus, what a creep! Miss, could I bother you a minute? Do you speak English?

L: Bother me? Oh, yes. I studied English at university.

J: Well, good for you. But could you tell me how I can get to the baggage return? I can't figure it out from all these signs. It's damned confusing.

L: No, it's not. I guess you're lucky they all speak English here. You go straight on and down the escalator. Just follow the signs. Where are you from?

J: St. Paul, Minnesota. Why do you ask?

L: I *have been to America *last year in Boston at a language school. Are you here for the language?

J: I'm here on business. I guess I won't be learning German. It's not an international language. Only fifty or sixty million people as far as I know.

L: That's wrong. A businessman shouldn't get his figures wrong. We're eighty million, as a matter of fact. We are a leading economic power.

J: Europe?

L: No, Germany, I mean.

J: Gee ma'am, this place is no bigger than California. I mean I'm sure

FOCUS ON GERMANY 6

it's very nice but ... Well, here's my card; just drop in for a drink when you are in the States again and we'll carry on our discussion.

L: Thank you for your *kidneys ... Mein Gott, ich stehe hier und vergesse die Zeit. Wiedersehen.

J: Well, what got into her? She just took off. Strange people!
(James goes to collect his baggage. After half an hour it still hasn't arrived. James finds his way to the lost property).

J: Excuse me, sir. I came on Air Lingus 452 from Dublin.

C: Einen Augenblick. Eins nach dem anderen. So jetzt sind Sie an der Reihe. Was haben wir für ein Problem?

J: I'm sorry. I don't speak German. Do you speak English?

C: A little. What is your problem?

J: Well, you see, I arrived at the airport but my luggage didn't get here. Air Lingus, flight 452.

C: But that is not possible. The airplane arrived one hour *before.

J: I know that. I was on it. But my baggage wasn't.

C: No, that's not possible. We would know these things.

J: Well excuse me, my baggage did not arrive. Are you calling me a liar?

C: Certainly not. Can I see your ticket please? Ah, Air Lingus from Dublin. That explains everything. Well, things like this happen with the smaller foreign airlines.

J: Look! I don't care which company was involved. What can you do about it? Can you check? Can you telephone someone?

C: One thing at a time. Would you please fill in these three forms first. Then we'll see what we can do for you.

J: *(after 10 minutes, meanwhile a new clerk has taken over)* Here are the forms. But where's your colleague? He gave me these forms here to fill in. My baggage hasn't arrived, you know.

C: My colleague? Oh you mean that student who helps out during the peak hours. Can I have your ticket, please? Well, let me see. Hmm. You have filled in the forms for Lufthansa passengers. This is not OK. For suitcases that get lost on foreign airlines you need one green and two pink forms. You get them in room 234 on the first floor. My colleague might still be in, if not come back to me.

J: Listen, this is supposed to be a major airport. You just find my baggage or I'm going to break a few bones around here.

Chapter 6

B Task 1: Train your brain

Look at the text again.
1. Which airline did James book to fly to Germany?
2. Why did he have to fill in three different forms?
3. Why did the first employee give him the wrong forms?

B Task 2: Going international – airport English

Asking for Information

Dürfte ich Sie kurz belästigen? ....

Ich habe mich hier verlaufen. ....

Können Sie mir sagen, wie ich
zur Gepäckausgabe komme? ....

Folgen Sie einfach den Schildern. ....

Mein Gepäck ist nicht mitgekommen. ....

B Task 3: Understanding American English (1)

Look again at the text and find the American English phrases.

I'll ask this man. ....

What a rude fellow! ....

Where's the baggage claim, please? ....

Excuse me, madam ... .

She's just run away. ....

FOCUS ON GERMANY 6

B   Watch their ways: How the Germans see themselves

Let's analyse what some Germans said to James at the airport.

How others see the Germans	How they see themselves
Wie bitte? Sorry, I'm in a hurry, my flight …. wurde aufgerufen.	
Germans are time-dominated, always in a hurry; punctuality is an obsession.	Time is central to our culture. Punctuality is a form of politeness.
For suitcases that get lost on foreign airlines you need one green and a two pink forms.	
They enjoy regulations and rigid rules. Germany is a bureaucrat's paradise.	True. We believe in good rules and regulations. They avoid problems and solve problems.
There's the plan of the airport over there. It explains the system. … It's simple, systematic and logical.	
They have systems and subsystems. Take the S-Bahn and the U-System: Which ticket covers which stretches? It's chaotic.	Systems make our world go round. There is nothing quite like having a system, even a complicated one.
That's wrong. A businessman should get his figures right.	
Germans are schoolmasters. They are blunt and direct. We would have said: "Are you sure that your figures are right?"	We say what we mean and mean what we say. In the Bible it says: Deine Rede sei ja, ja und nein, nein. Alles andere ist von Übel.

☺ Time to smile at the Germans

James Kelly asked a local[1] in Hollerberg: "Does this town have any nightlife?"– "Yes," replied the local, "but she's ill today."

---

1 Einheimischer

Chapter 6

B) Task 4: Typical German mistakes

They said	They should have said
You can become a plan at ... *become: werden*	.... *bekommen: ....*
I have been last year in Boston. *Zeit und Wortstellung!*	.... *Wie lautet die Regel?*
Thank you for your kidneys. *Ein typischer Wortfehler*	....

B) Task 5: Understanding American English (2)

Are you a linguistic genius? Can you tell American English from British English? The first example has been done for you.

Which is which?		AE / BE
1 a	Dave will blow his top.	X /
1 b	Our chairman might tend to disagree.	/ X
2 a	I'm not quite with you on that.	/
2 b	You're talking bullshit.	/
3 a	That's a beautiful scenario.	/
3 b	We might find a way of making that work.	/
4 a	Bean-counters drive me mad.	/
4 b	Accountants can be a nuisance.	/
5 a	Will they ever be a force in business again?	/
5 b	Will they ever come back from the grave?	/
6 a	You gotta be kidding.	/
6 b	Hm, that's an interesting idea.	/

FOCUS ON GERMANY 6

L) Letter from Germany

Hi Dave,

Still alive and kicking. I'm in Germany. I've had some discussions with a few people here. They seem to consider themselves to be the centre of things here in Europe. I guess we should try to score here.
On the other hand I don't see any difference to Britain over the water. You have to pay for every coffee. Breakfast is very weak. Just a roll with slices of sausage meat. This morning I asked for a glass of water at breakfast and, would you believe, I had to pay for it.
At present I'm in Heidelberg. We've got another golf course tomorrow. I'll be in a village near here. They've just built a huge golf course for local companies. I have a meeting with the owner. He's also CEO of S.U.P., a top software company here in Europe. I'll check it all out and phone you about the outcome tomorrow afternoon.

Yours Jamie

M) Mind your Manners

What you should not say to a German.
- → (At the swimming pool) That's my towel.
- → (At the Robinson club) You're lying on my deck-chair.
- → Excuse me, have you got a minute?
- → (On the motor way) Can you help me?
- → Tell us a joke.
- → (At the Frankfurt Car Fair) I like Japanese cars.
- → Was your father in the SS?
- → Want to hear the latest Hitler joke?

Chapter 6

Going international: Typical German

A market research firm, the Parkland Research Europe, carried out an opinion poll among 185 business executives, lawyers, engineers, teachers and other professional people from seven European countries. They published their findings in the Guide to National Practices in Western Europe. Here is a summary of what other nations thought of the Germans and the British.

Let us take the British first. The reactions were mixed. Some found them calm, stiff, reserved, open-minded and trustworthy. Others think they are hidebound and superior. Everyone was unanimous that they had an excellent sense of humour. The British themselves most admired the characters of the Dutch.

What about the Germans? Most Europeans agreed that the Germans had the highest proportion of good qualities. And the Germans, of course, liked themselves best of all nations. They considered themselves tolerant, but nobody else did. They saw themselves as fashionable. Others found them square. The Italians are dumbfounded by the German capacity to get things done without bribing anyone, but regard them as utterly lacking in style. The French regard the Germans with suspicion and a measure of loathing, and seek to contain them by chumming-up. To the Austrians a good German would be one who is far away – preferably across the Atlantic, or even further if they didn't depend on the deutschmarks of the German tourists that prevent their economy from collapsing.

The English have always had a high regard for German cleverness and thoroughness, somehow imagining that of all Europeans, the Germans are most like themselves. This illusion probably has its roots in the fact that so many Germans have occupied the British throne or been powers behind it.

The Germans regard the English as being very nice and mostly harmless, almost German. They respect the Swiss for their seriousness, honesty, punctuality and cleanliness – and they have never been to war with the Swiss. However, they like the Americans best. For the Germans, the United States is the headmaster in the school of nations.
More in: S. Zeidenitz, B.Barkow, *The Xenophobe's Guide to The Germans*

FOCUS ON GERMANY

B Task 6: Our country quiz: Ireland – Britain – Germany

A. How many adults can follow a discussion in a foreign language?

1. Let's first look at Ireland. What per cent of Irish adults speak

German	French?
a 15%	a 12%
b 7%	b 6%
c 2%	c 3%

2. What about Great Britain? What per cent of British adults speak

German	French?
a 24%	a 25%
b 12%	b 15%
c 6%	c 5%

3. And now to our country. How good are we at languages?

English	French
a 63%	a 38%
b 53%	b 28%
c 43%	c 18%

B. How strong are their economies?

1. Their birthrates will affect the size of their markets and the habits of their consumers. Which of the three countries has the highest and which the lowest birthrate?
2. There are only two countries within the European Union where the birth rate is higher than the death rate. Which are these countries?
3. What per cent of the German population will be under 20 years by the year 2030?

        a 36%   b 26 %   c 16%

4. How much more expensive is life in Germany compared to Greece?

        a by 60%   b 40 %   c 30 %

5. What about their gross national products (1992 in billion $)?

Ireland	Great Britain	Germany
a 48·73	a 618·8	a 761·8
b 38·73	b 518·8	b 661·8
c 18·73	c 418·8	c 561·8

Chapter 6

(V) Vocabulary to help you with the text

admire	bewundern
arrow	Pfeil
behaviour	Benehmen
blunt	ungehobelt; direkt, offen
brain	Gehirn
bribe someone	jemanden bestechen
capacity	Fähigkeit
chum-up with someone	sich mit jemandem anfreunden
collapse	zusammenbrechen
consider someone tolerant	jemanden für tolerant halten
contain an enemy	einen Feind im Zaum halten
deck-chair	Liegestuhl
depend on	abhängig sein von
dumbfounded	verblüfft
enjoy	mögen, genießen
escalator	Rolltreppe
executive	leitender Angestellter
fashionable	modisch, modern, elegant
findings	Ergebnisse, Erhebungen
form	Formblatt, Formular
get one's figures wrong	mit falschen Zahlen arbeiten
headmaster	Schuldirektor
hidebound	engstirnig, beschränkt, borniert
involved; be ~	beteiligt sein
kidney	Niere
kindness	Freundlichkeit
latest; the ~ joke	der neueste Witz
leading economic power	führende Wirtschaftsmacht
liar	Lügner
loathing	Abscheu
major airport	wichtiger Flughafen
market research	Marktforschung
opposite	Gegenteil
owner	Besitzer
peak hours	Stoßzeiten

FOCUS ON GERMANY

proportion	Anteil
preferably	vorzugsweise, am liebsten
punctuality	Pünktlichkeit
regard; have high ~ for	Hochachtung haben vor
regulations	Vorschriften
roll	Semmel, Brötchen
rude	grob, unhöflich
score	Erfolg haben, Treffer erzielen
seriousness	Ernsthaftigkeit
square	anständig, ehrlich
subsystem	Untersystem
suitcase	Koffer
superior	hier: überheblich
suspicion	Verdacht, Argwohn
towel	Handtuch
trustworthy	vertrauenswürdig

:) Hit them on the head

One German makes a philosopher, two a public meeting, three a war.
                        Robert MacDonald, Summit Conference, 1982

Why do Germans envy the Chinese?
Because they have still got their Wall.

Contrary to popular belief, the Germans do not know everything,
they just know everything better.

6 Chapter

B Our German crossword puzzle

Across: 3 Germany's publisher no. 1, 5 ? one's figures wrong, 6 repair the word: refurgis, 8 you dry your hands with it, 11 he got himself ? at the airport, 12 peak hours are ? hours, 14 American English for 'rude fellow', 17 part of James' golf balls, 18 James had to fill ? forms, 19 still Prime minister in 1997

Down: 1 Dave will blow his ?, 2 1 ? we should try to score here, 3 opposite of 'wrong', 4 you have to fill it in, 6 just ? in this form, please., 7 it's spoken in Ireland, 9 seafood, 10 British English for 'hassle', 13 you ? your bottom dollar, 15 English for 'heben, erhöhen', 16 top, highest point

Chapter 7

FOCUS ON GERMANY
Beeping balls for the board

Time for a grin

What German politicians say:
"Germany is not interested in dominating Europe ... "

And what some still think:
"... it's the world we are after."

Chapter 7

Meeting the members of the board

So Jamie spent a relaxing evening drinking apple wine and planning his meeting with S.U.P.

> At S.U.P. in the small conference room.
> Dr. Recht (**R**), Herr Blitz (**B**), James Kelly (**J**), Frau Nollet (**N**)

R: Gentlemen, I'd like to introduce Mr Kelly to you all. Mr Kelly has just arrived from the States.

B+N: How do you do?

J: Fine thanks. Well, let's forget all the formalities. Just call me Jamie. Well, if you don't object, I'd like to come straight to the point.

R: We share your opinion, Mr Kelly. Perhaps I could begin by explaining the tasks of the people present. I myself am the Managing Director of this modest software company. This is Mr Blitz who is responsible for Public Relations and Advertising. And last but not least Mrs Nollet, my personal assistant. She will take care of the minutes.

J: Hi, everybody.

R: Mr Kelly, could you give us an overview of what you can offer? Why do you think this golf-ball might interest us?

J: You bet it will. We've got a whole bunch of equipment which could make your company hum. You'll hum so much you'll be able to light up a football stadium.

B: I beg your pardon. We do not work with football. Our main activities include golf, tennis, badminton and squash.

J: I know, I know, anyhow let me just give you a short presentation of our company. Have you got an OHP handy? I ...

B: Sorry to interrupt you, Mr Kelly, but I'm afraid we haven't got enough time for the history of your company. We have naturally checked in detail all the data you sent us.

J: Well, gentlemen and ma'am. I didn't know that you had time to read the whole stuff ...

B: We agreed that you would explain to us only the advantages of your balls with a beep. Could we just keep to the subject, if you don't mind? Did you not receive our letter and brochures? We were afraid you might not get the package in time. America is such a vast country and ...

J: The pony express is still working fine. Of course I got the whole

FOCUS ON GERMANY 7

    package. I gather you've got a hell of a fine business going here. Anyhow, I'll come back to our SASL products. Here's our range ...

R: Sorry to interrupt you again, Mr Kelly. We have naturally checked your most impressive product range in detail in the last two weeks. But back to the matter. Please consider me as a sort of referee. Mr Blitz here will take care of purchasing details and the market potential. Mrs Nollet will take notes.

J: Well, thanks for your time gentlemen. Now let's come to our deal. I think I've got two babies here that will be of interest for you guys.

B: Could you explain them one at time, please?

J: Sure thing! I know what you mean. Everything in the right order. It reminds me of a story about a friend of mine. He had bought a pick-up and it broke down. He got real upset and phoned ...

R: I beg your pardon, Mr Kelly. Time is short. Perhaps we should concentrate on today's matter. We have another important meeting in 45 minutes.

J: *(getting a little nervous)* Right on! Sorry gents. Back to golf. Well, my first star is for your beginner golfer. It is a golf-ball with a beeper in it and ...

B: Interesting. But wouldn't that affect the weight? That is against the rules and regulations.

J: That's the beauty of it. By careful machining we've kept the weight the same. Your beginners won't have to waste their time and yours searching for hours for their balls.

B: I understand what you mean but I'm sure that searching is a part of the game of golf. What do you think about it, Herr Dr. Recht?

R: Perhaps our young friend has a point here. Time is money. Our clients, who are members of the board in one firm or another, have a problem with their time. Perhaps we can make a pilot project. If, of course, the quality meets our expectations.

J: Sure it will. Our balls have been tested in our specially designed Mark 4 computerised golf simulator. Sixty shots a minute, one ball a second. Beat that! Now, how many balls are you going to take, gentlemen? My special offer is ... let me see ... 3000 ...

B: Just a moment, young man. Could you give us more details about those simulated tests and then we might talk about your second hmm ... 'baby' as you put it ...

7 Chapter

B Task 1: Train your brain

How well can you read between the lines? Sometimes more than one answer might be correct.

1. What kind of company is S.U.P.?
   - **a** software company
   - **b** a sports club
   - **c** a public relations firm

2. What does Dr. Recht mean when he says "We share your opinion, Mr Kelly"?
   - **a** We Germans have a lot in common with the Americans.
   - **b** Formalities are a waste of time.
   - **c** What a blunt fellow you are.

3. What could Mr Blitz have meant by "We were afraid you might not have got the package"?
   - **a** I hope you haven't come to this meeting unprepared.
   - **b** Letters sometimes take weeks to cross the Atlantic.
   - **c** Postal service is slow in a big country like America.

4. James replies "The pony express is still working fine."
   - **a** In the far West, some postmen still come on horseback.
   - **b** Our postal service is well organised. You should know that.
   - **c** He means exactly what he says: "We've still got a fine pony express where I live."

5. "Could you first tell us more about those computer-simulated tests? And then we can talk about your second idea."
   - **a** In Germany we do business step by step.
   - **b** Before we take a decision we would like to get all the details.
   - **c** We are particularly interested in everything that has to do with computers.

FOCUS ON GERMANY 7

B Watch their ways in meetings and presentations (1)

Americans and Germans are closer to each other than both are to other nations. Let's see what they have in common.

1.	**Management**	The Germans have adopted the American scientific management theories.
2.	**Time**	No waste of time! Straight to the point.
3.	**Values**	Honesty is the basis of business.
4.	**Preparation**	They expect all participants to be well-prepared.
5.	**Etiquette**	Bluntness is preferred to subtlety.
6.	**Contract**	A signature is binding.
7.	**Americans seen by the Germans**	Americans think they are the greatest. Germans agree. They admire their success and know that America has always been 4-6 years ahead of Germany in everything.

B Task 2: Cross-cultural awareness test (1)

What do they have in common?
Here are some lines from the meeting. Put the number from the above table that explains best the following quotations.

a	We have naturally checked all the data you sent us in detail.	
b	Of course I got the whole package. You've got a hell of a fine business going here.	
c	Now straight to the point.	
d	I'm afraid we haven't got enough time for the history of your company.	
e	Your beginners won't waste their time searching for balls.	

☺ Time for a smile

Sign in a German shop: Never mind your German. We speak good broken English.

Chapter 7

B) Task 3: Understanding American English

British English	American English
You can be sure I will.	....
A whole lot of things.	....
Make something work well.	....
Certainly!	....
Sorry, gentlemen.	....

L) Watch their ways in meetings and presentations (2)

Nations differ as to the way they conduct meetings and presentations. James and Mr Blitz would have got along much better with each other if they had known about these cultural differences.

Meetings the American way

1. They start with humour, jokes, wisecracks.
2. They are quickly on first-name terms at the first meeting.
3. They want you to put your cards on the table at once; no beating about the bush.
4. Communication is a fight: they confront, provoke, they use sarcasm and kidding.
5. They are making an offer, and expect a counter-offer.
6. They want "yes" in principle; details can be settled later.
7. They tend to start with presentations listeners are not always prepared for.
8. The outcome: the instant deal; they wish to do the business as soon as possible.

Meetings the German way

1. They start with introductions and the agenda; no jokes.
2. They expect to be addressed with Herr and Doktor.
3. A meeting has a beginning, a middle and an end; one thing at a time, step by step.
4. Communication is explaining, asking questions, exchanging and testing views.
5. They are listening to arguments and replying with counter-arguments.
6. They want to settle the details first and then take a decision.
7. Everybody should come well-prepared. No surprises, no spontaneous presentations.
8. The outcome: they expect clarity and reliability. They need time to deliberate and test.

FOCUS ON GERMANY 7

B Task 4: Cross-cultural awareness test (2)

Here are some lines from the last meeting. Can you put the correct number from the list on page 90 plus A = American; G = German next to the quotation? The first one has been done for you.

It reminds me of a funny story about a friend of mine …	1A
Perhaps I could begin by explaining the tasks of the people present here.	
Let me just give you a short presentation of our company and our product range.	
A presentation of your company? Could we just keep to the subject, if you don't mind?	
What do you think about it, Herr Dr. Recht?	
Hi, everybody. Just call me Jamie.	
Could you explain them one at a time in detail?	
Now let's come to our deal.	
How many balls are you going to take? My special offer is …	
Just a moment, please. Could you first tell us more about those computer simulated tests?	

B Task 5: The hidden meaning. Philosopher's test (1)

What do they understand by individualism? Western countries belong to the individual leadership cultures. Individualism is one characteristic of the leader. Even such a basic concept can mean different things in different countries.

Can you match these statements against the following nations?

1. United States
2. Great Britain
3. Spain
4. Germany

a self-centredness (Ichbezogenheit)
b autonomy (Selbständigkeit)
c self-reliance (Selbstvertrauen)
d non-conformity (Andersartigkeit)

7 Chapter

L Watch their ways in meetings and presentations (3.

Meetings the American way	Meetings the German way
Americans are good listeners when a subject interests them.	Germans (and Swedes) are the best listeners of all European nations.
attention span: 30 minutes	attention span: 1 hour or more
They expect catch phrases and hard sell.	They expect lots of prints, figures, delivery dates etc.
They listen to be entertained.	They listen for information, ask questions to make sure they have understood correctly.
They want to be sold the product.	They are interested in the price.
They expect modernity, they want the short-term deal rather than a long-term relationship.	They expect solidity of the company and solidity of the product; they are interested in a business partnership.

B Task 6: The hidden meaning. Philosopher's test (2)

What do they understand by truth? For Germans (and Americans) the way to successful contracts is keeping to the truth, the absolute truth. This is not always the case with other nations. Even our closest neighbours see it differently.

Can you match these statements to the following nations?

	Nation		Attitude towards truth
1	Italy, France	a	There is no absolute truth.
2	Britain	b	Adherence to the truth must not destroy the harmony and balance of society.
3	Japan	c	The truth is the truth as long it doesn't rock the boat (create unnecessary problems).
4	China	d	Smooth social relationships are more important than the truth.

# FOCUS ON GERMANY 7

L) Letter from Germany

Dear Dave

You know I'm in Germany. Today I had a meeting with the boss of a golf-course at a local software company, S.U.P. Well, that was the tops. I hadn't even begun to show them our stuff before they interrupted me. They were quite rude. I could hardly get myself together. Anyway we parted friends. Dr. Recht turned out to be a quite different fellow as soon as he left the company. He took me to a restaurant and gave me some lessons about history and the German Reich, which means the German Commonwealth. They've had three so far, and they seem to be working on it.

The most important river is the Rhine, although it's only a trickle compared to the Potomac. France and Germany have been fighting over it for centuries because the legend goes that a hundred years ago or so one young Siegfried ran away with the all the gold reserves of the Niebelungen Bank and dumped them into the Rhine. Their FBI hasn't been able to catch him so far.

The Germans are a people of many contradictions. For example, they are crazy about cars. In East Germany they fancy Mercedes cars and Trabies. You don't know what a Trabie is? Well, it makes your average Skoda look like a Ferrari. They love their cars more than anything else. They keep their children indoors so that their cars can play in the streets. On Saturdays you can see them washing them. Only foreigners drive around in unwashed cars.

See you later.
James

P.S. I'm flying to Lisbon tomorrow. It's in a small state called Portugal.

Chapter 7

B Task 7: The travelling manager's country quiz

1. Which is the biggest country in the European Union?
    a Germany
    b Spain
    c France
2. What do most Germans understand by individual leadership?
    a self-centredness
    b autonomy
    c self-reliance
3. According to the British Social Attitudes Special International Report of 1989, the British are most proud of their monarchy. What were the Germans most proud of?
    a their culture
    b their 'Grundgesetz'
    c their economical achievement
4. Who dominates Germany's business?
    a the big German banks
    b German, American and Japanese multi-national companies
    c the government, the trade unions and the middle-sized companies
5. What is English for "Aufsichtsrat"?
    a management board
    b board of directors
    c supervisory board
6. Which businessmen think that German managers are too slow to arrive at a business contract?
    a Americans and Australians
    b British and French
    c Japanese and Arabs
7. What do other nations think of German advertising?
    a the pictures have little to do with the product
    b it gives a lot of detailed product information, therefore it is not visual enough and a bit boring
    c striking illustrations and a lot of clever slogans

FOCUS ON GERMANY 7

(V) Vocabulary to help you with the text

above; the ~ table	die obige Tabelle
adherence to the truth	Festhalten an der Wahrheit
adopted theories	übernommene Theorien
attention span	Aufmerksamkeitsspanne
average	Durchschnitt(s-)
beat about the bush	auf den Busch klopfen
bluntness	schonungslose Offenheit
boring	langweilig
break (broke, broken) down	eine Panne haben
conduct meetings	Besprechungen leiten
contradictions	Widersprüche
deal	Geschäft
deliberate	beraten
dump	versenken
entertain	unterhalten, bewirten
honesty	Ehrlichkeit
include	umfassen, einschließen
items	Artikel, Punkte
kidding	Spaß machen
light a stadium	ein Stadion beleuchten
machine something	etwas herstellen, be-, verarbeiten
make something hum	etwas in Schwung bringen
market potential	Marktchancen; Marktpotential
meet someone's expectations	jemandes Erwartungen erfüllen
member of the board	Vorstandsmitglied
minutes	Protokoll
part friends	als Freunde auseinandergehen
participant	Teilnehmer
prefer	vorziehen, lieber tun
prints	Druckerzeugnisse
product range	Produktpalette
proud; be ~ of	stolz sein auf
purchase	Einkauf
receive information	Informationen empfangen

Chapter 7

referee	Schiedsrichter; Berichterstatter
reliability	Zuverlässigkeit
rock the boat	die Sache gefährden
search for something	nach etwas suchen
settle details	Einzelheiten regeln
share someone's opinion	jemandes Meinung teilen
subtlety	Feinheit, Spitzfindigkeit
matter; to the ~	zur Sache
trickle	Rinnsal
truth	Wahrheit
upset; get ~	sich beunruhigen, aufregen
visual	bildhaft
wisecrack	Witz

☺ Hit them on the head

The Ossie guards who used to be employed at the Wall to keep people in, have had to be reassigned[1] to patrol the Eastern border[2] to keep people out.

Zeidenitz, Barkow

Emperor Charles V (1500 -1558) on European languages:
> To God I speak Spanish,
> to women Italian,
> to men French,
> and to my horse German.

---

1 wiedereinsetzen 2 Grenze

FOCUS ON PORTUGAL
Big deal with Sporty-Rest

Chapter 8

The truth about meetings

A meeting should consist of three men,
two of whom are absent.

If you cannot convince[1] them, confuse[2] them.
If you want to get along[3], go along[4].

Negotiation is a process in which both sides win.

---

1 überzeugen 2 verwirren 3 auskommen (mit) 4 zustimmen

Chapter 8

Big deal with Sporty-Rest

James Kelly arrives at his hotel in the old part of Lisboa (Lisbon). The reason for his trip is to get into contact with Sporty-Rest, a group of holiday clubs which specialize in offering tourists who come to Portugal from all over Europe easy sport with a hotel stay. Well, you can forget the word talent. But they're people, too. Anyway there is James. And there are the representatives of Sporty-Rest.

> At the Sporty-Rest head office in Lisbon.
> Present: Manual Gonzales (**M**), Paolo Gonzales (**P**), Dr. Juan Sines (**S**), James Kelly (**J**), who has been waiting for about 20 minutes for the meeting to begin.

M: Gentlemen, I must apologise for being late, but it has been one of those days, you know. I'd like to introduce you to Mr James Kelly, from America.

All: How do you do?

J: Hi. James is my ... ehm ... I'm James Kelly from SASL.

M: As for my humble self, I'm responsible for purchasing in our team. Mr. Gonzales, my brother by the way, is the majority shareholder of our little group, and Dr. Sines, our brother-in-law, is in charge of publicity.

P: Well, we've spent some time reading your information about your very interesting products. Of course, we couldn't quite understand all the potential and advantages which your equipment offers.

J: Of course not, sir. Where would you like me to begin?

M: That's entirely up to you. You are the specialist. Well, perhaps you could give us a brief overview of what you consider might be most useful and successful here in our environment?

J: That'll be my pleasure. If I might just describe the situation as I see it. Here in your state your group consists of ten Sporty-Rest hotels located all over the country. Five are in the south in the Algarve which is very hot, about 35° to 40° for four to five months a year. And you have several types of sports which you offer to your customers. And by the way, ninety-five percent of your clients are from abroad. I reckon that's about it.

P: I see you've done your homework.

FOCUS ON PORTUGAL

J: Yes sir, because it's in your interest and your interest is our interest, too.

M: Well, we're certainly excited to hear what you have to tell us.

J: You're so well distributed across this State ...

S: Country. Mr Kelly! Portugal is a country and and we do not have a federal system yet although some people would like it.

J: Sorry gents, just a slip in terminology. As I was saying you have a wide spread. We'd suggest a package of several of our lines together. For example, our line of collapsible golf clubs for your three golf hotels; the special tennis and squash rackets for your sites in Porto and in the north.

P: And if we have understood your excellently illustrated documentation correctly all your devices give special support to the sports learner who is not so talented.

J: You've hit the bull's eye. Now ...
(Mr Manuel's secretary slips in and whispers something to Senhor Manuel Gonzales. He gets up and leaves the room. James is confused and gets up as well)
What's the matter? If I said anything to offend you, gentlemen ... the bull's eye means ...

P: Oh no, Mr Kelly, that's perfectly all right. If you'll excuse me please, I'll be back in a minute.

S: If I might come in at this point, these products seem to be interesting, but do you have something else that would help Sporty-Rest to stand out from the rest? My little joke. Ha ha.

J: Yes, Dr. Sines. I was just about to throw my ace down. It's this. Five of your hotels are located near to hilly landscape. What's a simple sport that we can offer in those sort of places?

M: Hill walking?

J: Well, we don't actually supply mechanical legs for the weary walker. No gents, the mountain bike for bikers who can't cycle any more.

P: And what is special about the bike?

J: It has special features. The handle bars are fitted out with instruments to show your heartbeat, blood pressure, distance travelled. It's got a pager built-in so if you suddenly get tired the hotel can send a car to pick you up. And ... *(fade out)*.
(fade in) ... so that' about it.

Chapter 8

P: Well, thank you, Mr Kelly. This has been most informative. Oh, one other thing before you leave us. Is your company willing to provide us with trainers for all these devices?

J: Trainers? Hmm ... Well. I'm sure a training program can be worked out.

P: And we would hope that you would support us with the publicity for all your systems, in English, of course.

J: Oh, I'm not. ...

S: Of course this would be a national level campaign. As you say, it is in both our interests.

J: Wow, yes, of course, gents, just leave it to me.

P: Just for your information, we'll make a protocol of what we've discussed today. We prefer to have everything in the written form for the sake of clarity. A copy will be sent to you.

B Task 1: Train your brain

1. What does James mean by "You've a wide spread"?
    a You've hotels all over the country.
    b You offer a great variety of sports.
    c You get tourists from all over the world.
2. What is special about the mountain bike James has to offer?
    a It is for people who have an artificial leg.
    b The hotel can locate and pick up a guest in case of trouble.
    c It adapts to the guest's heart beat and blood pressure.
3. Why do the Portuguese ask James for support?
    a Their staff cannot show guests how to handle the equipment.
    b They need native speakers of English to write the adverts.
    c They are excellent negotiators who know how to keep costs down.

M Mind your manners

What you should not say to a Portuguese.
→ I thought you were Spanish.
→ The Portuguese make the best servants.
→ Name me three famous Portuguese.
→ You've got a real fine club in Real Madrid.

FOCUS ON PORTUGAL

B Watch their ways

1. They are not very touchy about national honour, religion, race.
2. They are more formal than the Spanish. They address anyone who appears qualified or intelligent as Duotor or Engenheiro.
3. They avoid conflicts with colleagues and business partners.
4. They are friendly, cheerful and communicative even at the beginning of a relationship.
5. Business is not done step by step. They are often involved in several tasks at a time.

L Watch their ways in meetings

The Portuguese way of doing business is different from the American, English or German way.

1. Management	Medium-sized companies are often run by members of a family or close friends.
2. Time	Don't be late, but be prepared to have to wait up to two hours.
3. Etiquette	It is not seen as impolite to leave in the middle of a meeting to deal with other jobs.
4. Strategy	They are clever negotiators: 1. They believe they are smarter, but try to appear the opposite. 2. They are very flexible. 3. They keep what they really want to the end.
5. Mentality	They are formal, but friendly and polite. They are quick, often opportunistic.
6. Preparation	They expect everybody to be well-prepared.
7. Minutes	Everything is put down in writing to avoid later misunderstandings.
8. Contract	Contrary to other latin or Asian countries a signature is binding.

Chapter 8

Task 2: Cross-cultural awareness test (1)

Here are some lines from the last meeting. Can you put the correct number from the list on page 101 next to the quotation?

Just for your information, we'll make a protocol of what we've discussed today.	
J: Where would you like me to begin? M: That's entirely up to you. You are the specialist.	
Of course we couldn't quite understand ... the advantages which your equipment offers.	
Oh, one other thing before you leave us ...	
... but do you have something else that would help Sporty-Rest to stand out from the rest?	

Task 3: Cross-cultural awareness test (2)

Here are some quotations which we think are typical of Americans (A), Germans (G), English (E), Portuguese (P).

Put the right letter next to the line.

Sorry to interrupt you, but I'm afraid we haven't got enough time for the history of your company. Let's keep to the subject.	
Well, perhaps you could give us a brief overview of what you consider might be most useful and successful here in our environment?	
I quite like that little device, however I'm not absolutely sure that this type of instrument will be of any use to our clients.	
We've got a whole bunch of equipment which could make your company hum. You'll hum so much you'll be able to light up a football stadium.	

☺ Food for thought

Those who are unable to learn from past meetings
have to repeat them.

FOCUS ON PORTUGAL

B Task 4 : Patch work

excuse		would hope		consider
	excited		apologise for	
humble self		perfectly		correctly
	homework		documentation	

The Portuguese are good orators. Can you complete these elegant sentences?

We've spent some time reading your .... about your very interesting products.

We're certainly .... to hear what you have to tell us.

I must .... being late, but it has been one of those days.

And we .... that you would support us with the publicity.

As for my .... I'm responsible for purchasing.

I see you've done your ....

Perhaps you could give us a brief overview of what you .... might be most useful here in our environment?

If we have understood your excellent documentation .... all your devices give support to the learner who is not so talented.

Oh no, Mr Kelly, that's .... all right.

If you'll .... me please, I'll be back in a minute.

☺ Time for a smile: A happy misunderstanding

An ageing millionairess was the first client to practise with the collapsible golf club at Sporty-Rest. The new young American trainer dramatically improved her technique. "Young man" she exclaimed, „I insist on making you a present to show you my gratitude" – "Well, if you insist", the pro replied, "you can buy me some golf clubs." The next week he received a telex: "Have bought you Wentworth and Sunningdale but St. Andrews refused to sell."

Chapter 8

(L) Letter from Portugal

Hi Dave,

Wow, it's certainly warm down here in the state of Portugal. Actually, they don't have states here like at home. It's a country about the size of a county back home in the US.

The people down here are very charming and they know what they want. Clever talkers, too.

They're a bit odd in their eating habits though. I haven't seen a good steak since I've been here. Only fish, fish and more fish. Still everybody to his own.

The hotel chain was very interested in our package. I've set up a deal, real king-size. Then at the very end of the discussion they dropped a bombshell. They insisted that we should bear the costs of the total advertising for the equipment and training programs. But the deal's big enough.

Sometimes I feel a bit out of things. The Europeans certainly seem very cultured. But I'm trying to roll with the punches.

Tomorrow I'm flying to Barcelona, Spain.

See you,
James

☺ Time for a smile: Hell on Earth

There have been many definitions of hell, but for the English the best definition is that it is a place where the Germans are the police, the Swedish are the comedians, the Italians are the defence force, Frenchmen dig the roads, the Belgians are the pop singers, the Spanish run the railways, the Turks cook the food, the Irish are the waiters, the Greek run the Government and the common language is Dutch.

David Frost and Antony Jay, *To England with Love*

FOCUS ON PORTUGAL

 **Going international:
Getting to know the Portuguese**

They are different from the Spanish. If the Portuguese people were not very different from the Spanish, Portugal would not exist. The Portuguese are an Atlantic nation, the Spanish are a Mediterranean nation. Until the 1974 revolution Portugal looked towards Africa (Angola, Mozambique) and South Africa. Their relationship with Brazil is very strong since they have a language in common. The contrast with Spain is startling. The Portuguese like things in writing. Well-expressed documents help to avoid uncertainty and misunderstandings. Contrary to other Latins they are good speakers of the English language, they expect to pay and be paid promptly. National honour is not a major factor. They are not touchy about race, religion or colour. They are less emotional than the Italians or the Spanish.

Ownership. The 1974 revolution was followed by the nationalisation of banking and industry. Since 1989 both sectors have gradually been reprivatised, but the state still owns fifty percent in the big enterprises and about a dozen rich families dominate the rest. Leadership and power are concentrated at the top of an organization based on personal family ties, loyalty and friendship.

Meetings. Meetings and appointments should be prepared by letter but don't expect a reply. Follow it up by phone. Letters and phone calls should be addressed to the boss of the company and not to the head of a department. Meetings are more for briefing and discussion than for getting clear results. They are not considered an appropriate forum for decision making or the delegation of tasks. Everybody is free to express his point of view and normally they disagree on principle. If, however, a senior person is present, he will dominate the discussion.

The agenda. Meetings normally start with some small talk. Don't ask questions about the revolution, don't praise their neighbour, Spain. Keep to the beauty of the country, their successful football team Benefica Lisboa or the Portuguese Shakespeare, the author Luis de

Chapter

Camoes. There will be an agenda, but people will not feel bound by it and may leave for other more pressing business. The Portuguese are a multi-tasking people, that is they think of and deal with several jobs at a time. This accounts for the fact that most appointments are unlikely to start on time – one reason why making and receiving telephone calls at home is common and often necessary for missed appointments during the day.

Negotiating. They come to the negotiation well informed about all aspects of the transaction. They know what they want from the start, but will tell you as late as they can in a negotiation. Unlike German negotiators, they are very flexible as to the route they will take to achieve their goal. They are, in fact, among the best negotiators in the world. Maybe that is why they obtained better terms for their entry into the Common Market than the Spanish. Centuries of trading with India, Africa and the Far East have taught them to be flexible, realistic and good losers.

Adapted from Richard D. Lewis, *When Cultures Collide*

(V) Vocabulary to help you with the text

account; this ~s for	dies ist eine Erklärung für
achieve a goal	ein Ziel erreichen
advantage	Vorteil
apologise	sich entschuldigen
appropriate forum	angemessene Plattform
artificial leg	künstliches Bein, Prothese
avoid misunderstandings	Mißverständnisse vermeiden
blood pressure	Blutdruck
brief overview	kurzer Überblick
briefing	Informationsveranstaltung
brother-in-law	Schwager
built-in	eingebaut

FOCUS ON PORTUGAL

clarity; for the sake of ~	um der Klarheit willen
consider	halten für, betrachten, erwägen
consist of	bestehen aus
contrary to	im Gegensatz zu
county	Landkreis
describe the situation	die Lage schildern
distribute	verteilen
environment	Gegend, Milieu, Umgebung
everybody to his own	jedem das Seine
federal system	bundesstaatliches System
feel bound	sich verpflichtet fühlen
gents (AE)	meine Herren
goal	Ziel
good loser	guter Verlierer
gradually	nach und nach
handle bars	Lenkrad
heartbeat	Herzschlag
hilly landscape	hügelige Landschaft
hit the bull's eye	den Nagel auf den Kopf treffen
humble	bescheiden, demütig
in charge of; be ~	verantwortlich sein für, leiten
line	hier: Sortiment, Reihe
located	gelegen
majority shareholder	Hauptaktionär
mechanical legs	mechanische Beine
medium-sized company	mittelständischer Betrieb
multi-tasking; be ~	mit mehreren Aufgaben gleichzeitig beschäftigt sein
national level campaign	landesweiter Feldzug
negotiator	Unterhändler, Verhandlungsführer
obtain better terms	bessere Bedingungen aushandeln
odd	sonderbar
offend	beleidigen
pager	Piepser
pick someone up	jemanden abholen, auflesen
praise (n.;v.)	Lob; loben

Chapter 8

provide someone with trainers	jemanden mit Lehrern versorgen
reckon	der Meinung sein
reply (n.;v.)	Antwort; antworten
responsible for	verantwortlich für
site	Gelände; hier: Anlage
slip (in terminology)	sich versprechen
smart	schlau, klug
stand out from the rest	sich von allen anderen abheben
startling	hier: verblüffend
successful	erfolgreich
supply	liefern
support; give ~ to someone	jemanden unterstützen
target; be right on ~	den Nagel auf den Kopf treffen
throw one's ace down	seinen Trumpf ausspielen
ties; family ~	Familienbande
touchy ; be ~ about	empfindlich gegen
variety	Vielfalt
weary walker	müder Wanderer
wide spread	große Verbreitung

☺ Time for a smile

James Kelly is the sort of American who would call John the Baptist[1] Jack[2].

---

1 Johannes der Täufer 2 umgangssprachlich für John

Chapter 9

FOCUS ON SPAIN
Boards and rods for the weak

🙂 Time for smile

It was late when James went into a Lisbon travel agency to book a hotel room in Barcelona. The employee handed him a complicated form to fill in[1]. "Oh, I can't be bothered with this now," James said. "I'm too tired. Fill it in for me, will you? My name is on the luggage label[2]."
The employee nodded, looked at the suitcase and wrote on the line next to 'Name of guest': Señor Genuine Pigskin[3].

---

1 ausfüllen 2 Namensschild am Koffer 3 echtes Schweinsleder

Chapter 9

Boards and rods for the weak

Jamie has arrived in Barcelona. He is one of those young Americans who is trying to learn quickly. ("The Spanish more or less live in the same country as the Portuguese so I'll deal with them the same way.") Let's see how our young friend gets on. His brief is to sell several interesting things to Pedro Barca, an elderly millionaire and owner of an ocean-side sports hotel complex near Tarragona. We find ourselves in a good restaurant, would you believe?

> In the restaurant: James (**J**), Don Pedro (**P**) and
> Don Pedro's secretary and assistant, the beautiful Gabriella (**G**).

J: Yes, I was over on the other side of your peninsula, in Portugal. Beautiful country.

P: Yes, of course, but unfortunately history hasn't granted us ownership of that charming place yet. Well, what may we offer you to drink? I suppose as an American you would prefer a coke?

J: Well, heck no! I just love your rosé wine. I'll take a ..., what's its name? Ah yes, Mateus Rosé!

G: Excuse me, Mr Kelly. That's not one of ours. It's made by our ... hmm ... brothers in Portugal. We have many good wines, too.

J: Oh gosh! I bet you do. Well, anything you suggest, Señor Barca. Wow, am I hungry!

P: I think I would suggest Paella before you choose something Portuguese.

J: That's great! I got real hungry. I was here at 12.30. I guess that's when we had our appointment, didn't we Señorita Gabriella?

G: We are so sorry, Mr Kelly. We were kept by unforeseen circumstances.

P: Don't take it too seriously. We were only one hour late. Ah, my charming Gabriella, what can I persuade you to drink today? Let me choose ... *(One hour later)*

P: Yes, that was a delicious meal. Ah, there's something I must settle on the phone. I will return in fifteen minutes or so. Excuse me.

J: Jesus, where's Pedro going now? I wanted to get down to business.

G: In Spain lunch is the time for food and conversation. What is your English saying? "All work and no play makes James a dull boy."

FOCUS ON SPAIN

J: It's Jack actually. Ah, here comes Señor Barca.
P: Let's have a final coffee together. We'll make an exception today - no siesta Gabriella. Now what has our friend to sell us?
J: You're sure you've had enough to eat? Okay, then if you're sitting comfortably, I'll begin. Your hotel is into water sports, isn't it?
P: Well, it's next to the water actually.
J: And the water supports your guests and we'll support them, too. We've got just the goodies to make your day, Señor Barca. Just take wind-surfing. We have some special gadgets that'll solve problems. Remember, we're SASL "Sports Aids for the Slow Learner".
P: What on earth are you talking about?
J: You're on your board, out in the sea. What is your main worry?
P: Getting back. Getting tired. Getting sun-burned.
J: There's a real merman. Exactly right. So we've got the answers. Our surfboards have a built-in compass system which locks onto land and guides you back. And when you're very tired and think it's the end of you, there's our marvelous super-powerful two-stroke surf-board motor, and we provide special sun-protectors, too, – all with no extra weight.
P: Well, you do surprise me, James.
J: What do you say? Do we get down to making a few calculations?
P: Oh, you're much too quick for us, James. Tell us, have you any more surprises?
J: You bet your bottom dollar. Heard of fish?
P: Well, we do eat them now and again.
J: And you've got to catch 'em, too. Look at this rod, the power-liner for the fisherman with a weak arm. This motor shoots your hook and line twice the distance. That's the way to land a big one, isn't it? ... Hey, why are you two laughing?

☺ Time for a smile

"How long has old Pedro been fishing?" - "I'm not sure, but he's the only member of the angling club fishing with a Louis XV rod[1]."

....

1 Angelrute

Chapter 9

B Task 1: Train your brain

1. What is James' surfboard equipped with?
- **a** a line locked onto the land to guide the surfer back
- **b** a small motor and a compass
- **c** two-stroke paddles

2. What is special about the fishing rod?
- **a** It is equipped with a weak arm to throw hook and line.
- **b** It is a Louis XV rod.
- **c** It is equipped with a device to shoot the line.

3. Why is Pedro making "an exception" today?
- **a** He is ready to talk business in a restaurant.
- **b** He is going to have his siesta.
- **c** He is settling something on the phone.

L One peninsula - two nations

Spain	Portugal
The Spanish are a Mediterranean nation.	The Portuguese are an Atlantic nation.
They think the Iberian Peninsula is Spanish.	They see the Spanish as potential invaders.
They are less formal. They use the *tu* form all over the place.	They are more formal. They use the titles.
The written document is not their strong point.	They expect well-written documents.
Personal dignity is more important than time or money. Do not make them lose face.	National honour, race, and religion are not major factors.
They are 'machos'.	They are less robust.
They like physical and eye contact.	They are more reserved.

FOCUS ON SPAIN

B Task 2: Cross-cultural awareness test (1)

1. What did James say that his Portuguese friends would not have liked?
2. Which remark might have offended a Spanish person?
3. What is the Spanish attitude towards Portugal?
4. Can you find anything in the dialogue that is typical of both the Spanish and the Portuguese?
5. Señor Barca addresses James Kelly by his first name. James addresses Pedro Barca, as Señor Barca, but his secretary as Señorita Gabriella. What is your comment?

M Mind your manners

What you should not to say to a Spaniard.
- → Up the Basques.
- → Gibraltar is British!
- → What did you do under Franco?
- → Spanish girls make the best chambermaids.
- → Now I understand why Picasso preferred to stay in France.

B Task 3: Pitfalls for marketing managers (1)

Here are two examples of advertising campaigns that were flops in Spanish speaking countries. Can you imagine why?

1. Parker Pens' slogan: 'Prevent embarrassment - use Parker Ink' was not a good idea. Why not?
2. And General Motors had to change the name of their *Nova* for Spanish speaking markets. Why?

☺ Time for a smile

James was watching some Spanish fishermen as they were preparing to go fishing. "What are those things on the beach?", he asked. "Lobster pots[1]," said the fisherman. "Gosh," exclaimed James, "Do you mean to say you've trained them to sit on those pots?"

....
1 Hummerkästen

Chapter 9

B Task 4: Cross-cultural awareness test (2)

Journalists organised a competition to write an article about elephants. Here are the titles. Can you match titles against nationalities?

Title of article	Nationality
1. How to breed bigger and better elephants	a English
2. The origin and development of the Indian elephant in the years 1200 - 1978	b French
3. The love life of elephants in central Africa	c German
4. How we sent an elephant to the moon	d American
5. Hunting Elephants in East Africa	e Spanish
6. Techniques of Elephant Fighting	f Russian

B Task 5: Pitfalls for marketing managers (2)

Advertising campaigns can backfire if the marketing manager is not familiar with the country. Here are two more problems for you to solve.

1. In the 1980s, Ford had to rename their *Fiera*. Why?
2. Ford was launching its *Caliente*, a new model designed for the Mexican market. They had to find a different name. Why?

☺ Time for a smile

SASL has been expanding[1] on the home market. That is why Dave invited two of his sales team into his office. "You have done so well with selling that I'm giving you each a cheque for $1,500", he said and after second thoughts[2] he added, " ... and if you keep on working like this, I might even sign[3] it."

---

1 wachsen, expandieren 2 nach einiger Überlegung 3 unterschreiben

FOCUS ON SPAIN

 Going international: Business etiquette for Spain

Handshakes and all that. Shake hands when first meeting, but not at following meetings, or when finally departing. Wait for a woman to offer her hand first. The Spanish are less formal than the Portuguese. They call their maid and the doorman *usted* (*Sie*) and their colleagues *tu* (*du*). In Latin America it is the other way round. Don't try to do business during afternoon siesta. Business lunch starts at about 13:30 and can last until 17:00. Dinner is between 22:00 and 23:00. Be careful not to get drunk. Dress conservatively.

Bosses. The quality most admired in a leader is courage. Consulting employees before decision-making may be interpreted as weakness and causes insecurity among the employees. The Spanish are a proud and independent nation. Like the torero in the arena, the senior executive makes his decisions on his own and uses the meeting to communicate his instructions. The Spanish like to be independent and make decisions on their own.

Management. Forecasting and planning are not typical features of Spanish business practice. Fixing a strategy is the responsibility of the chief executive or the owner. It will be based on intuition and business sense rather than on systematic study. Time spent gathering facts and figures and making studies is seen as time wasted. Accounting systems are designed to conceal information from tax authorities and banks.

Meetings. They are social occasions where everybody is expected to show great respect for the dignity of the others. Although most companies have introduced the American philosophy on how to run a company, the idea that a meeting can be used to decide on a plan of action, allocate responsibilities and coordinate implementation, is something that is not part of the Spanish mentality. Americans and Germans who are used to producing a result in which everyone will share the responsibility, will find this frustrating.

Invitations. If invited into the home, a gift is not expected, but you may bring a box of candy. Do not send flowers except for special occasions.

Conversations. Demonstrate interest in the country's history and culture. If you don't care for bullfighting and it comes up in conversation avoid criticism. The Spanish consider it an art to confront a massive animal that has been trained to kill man, with a little sword and a red cape. The typical English fox hunt is seen as a cowardly sport: the ladies and gentlemen sit safely astride a horse while their dogs tear small foxes to pieces.

Sources: J. Mole *Mind Your Manners* and D. Launay, *The Xenophobe's Guide to the Spanish*

Watch their ways

Mono-tasking and multi-tasking nations

The managers who James has been dealing with in the European Community so far can be divided into two different categories according to their work ethic. On the one hand, there are mono-tasking, target-orientated planners: English, Germans and French. They complete a task before they take up the next, they work according to schedules and concentrate on one job at a time.

On the other hand, there are the multi-tasking Portuguese, Spaniards and Italians who are more flexible. They are often busy with several jobs at a time. Furthermore, they are people-orientated. Conversation is more important than time-tables. That is why they are often late.

When 'mono-taskers' and 'multi-taskers' meet, conflicts are bound to arise, unless one party adapts to the other. Spaniards see no harm in leaving in the middle of a meeting to make an urgent phone call. Americans and Germans get angry when meetings drag on endlessly.

People-orientated and target-orientated nations

The Spanish are different from Germans, British or Americans who get frustrated when at the end of a negotiation there is no result. Since they are people-orientated, they are less interested in facts, figures and dead-

FOCUS ON SPAIN

lines. Instead of listening to a presentation, they watch the presenter: "Do we like them? Are they trustworthy? Are they the kind of people we want to do business with?" And when they like them, business will follow automatically. 'Mono-taskers' tend to think their Mediterranean partners are unreliable when they don't observe agendas, change plans or break contracts. An Italian or Spaniard doesn't see any sense in following plans when the situation has changed.

B Task 6 : Cross-cultural awareness test (3.

And now the test. The German (G) and the Spanish (S) are representatives of the two different types of businessmen. Do you recognise them? The first two have been done for you.

He or she ...		He or she ...	
works fixed hours	G	changes plans if necessary	
is impatient	S	is extrovert	
brief on the phone		separates job and private life	
rarely writes memos		works step by step	
contacts top key persons		works any hours	
argues logically		contacts head of department	

Source: R. L. Lewis *When Cultures Collide*

☺ Time for a smile

Dave Makeit, boss of SASL, asked the new secretary: "Have you posted those two parcels[1] I gave you? You know, the clubs to Ireland and the balls to Detroit." "I have", she said, "and what's more, I put right that mistake you made with the postage.[2]" "How do you mean?" asked the boss surprised. "Well, you put $15.20 worth of stamps on the local parcel and only a stamp for two dollars on that parcel to Ireland. But don't worry, I sorted it out[3]. I just changed the addresses."

---

1 Paket 2 Porto 3 in Ordnung bringen

Chapter 9

B Task 7: The travelling manager's country quiz

1. Salaries of top managers differ considerably in Europe. Can you match country and salary?

Country (1992)	Salary in pounds/year
1) Britain	a 110, 000
2) France	b 98,000
3) Italy	c 125,000
4) Germany	d 105,000
5) Switzerland	e 123,000
6) Spain	f 87,000

2. How often have Spaniards gone to the polls since the referendum in 1976? More than

    a 70   **b** 50   **c** 30   **d** 20 times

3. Who are these letters addressed to?
   a Muy Sr. mio
   b Esmo Senhor Rodrigo

4. What do the Spaniards spend most of their money on?
   a furniture, carpets
   b electrical household equipment
   c clothes

5. There is not one Spain, but several Spains. Which are not Spanish?
   a Catalonians   **d** Galicians
   b Basques   **e** Andalousians
   c Extranjeros   **f** Catalans

6. What do the Spanish prefer to drink? Wine or beer?

7. What is the attitude of the Spanish towards beggars?
   a they are ashamed that poverty exists in Spain
   b they treat them with respect

FOCUS ON SPAIN 9

(V) Vocabulary to help you with the text

accounting system	Buchhaltungssystem
advertising campaign	Werbefeldzug
allocate responsibility	Verantwortung zuweisen
astride; sit ~ a horse	hoch zu Roß sitzen
attitude towards	Einstellung gegenüber
backfire	nach hinten losgehen
be into water sports	Wassersport mögen
beggar	Bettler
bound; problems are ~ to arise	Probleme müssen auftreten
breed	züchten
brief	Anweisungen
bullfighting	Stierkampf
chambermaid	Zimmermädchen
conceal	verbergen
comment	Kommentar
competition	Wettbewerb
considerably	beträchtlich
courage	Mut
cowardly	feige
delicious	köstlich
departure	Abschied, Abreise
differentiate	unterscheiden
dignity	Würde
distance	Entfernung, Abstand
elderly; ~ millionaire	ein älterer Millionär
equipped with	ausgestattet mit
exception	Ausnahme
feature	Eigenschaft, Merkmal
gadget	Gerät
go to the polls	zur Wahlurne gehen
goodies	Bonbons; klasse Sachen
grant	gewähren
have in common	etwas gemeinsam haben
Iberian Peninsula	Iberische Halbinsel

Chapter 9

implementation	Durchführung, Umsetzung
independent	unabhängig
instructions	Anweisungen
invader	Eindringling
launch	auf den Markt bringen
lock onto	(Ziel) erfassen und verfolgen
Mediterranean	Mittelmeer-
mono-tasking; be ~	jeweils nur mit einer Sache beschäftigt sein
multi-tasking; be ~	mit mehreren Aufgaben gleichzeitig beschäftigt sein
offend	beleidigen
origin	Ursprung, Herkunft
persuade	überreden
physical contact	Körperkontakt
prefer	vorziehen, lieber tun
pregnancy	Schwangerschaft
prevent embarrassment	Peinlichkeiten vermeiden
rod	Rute
settle something on the phone	etwas per Telefon regeln
suggest	vorschlagen
support	unterstützen; hier: tragen
take it seriously	es ernst nehmen
trustworthy	vertrauenswürdig
two-stroke motor	Zweitaktmotor
unforeseen circumstances	unvorhergesehene Umstände
unreliable	unzuverlässig
unsuitable	unpassend, ungeeignet
Up the Basques!	Es leben die Basken!
used; be ~ to	gewohnt sein zu
weight	Gewicht

FOCUS ON SPAIN

🙂 Hit them on the head

If God were not God he would be King of Spain.

Three Spaniards, four opinions.

The smoke of my country shines more than the fire of others.
Proverb

The Spanish do not particularly differentiate between Austrians, Germans, Dutch, Chinese, Italians or Japanese. All are *extranjeros,* foreigners.

The Spanish are noisy, having no consideration for others, always late for appointments if they turn up at all, and never seeming to go to bed except in the afternoon.

The most important word in their language is *mañana* and this means 'tomorrow' or 'some time tomorrow' or 'maybe next week', 'possibly next year', 'sometime' or 'never ever'.
Drew Launay, A Xenophobe's Guide to the Spanish

Chapter 9

B Our Spanish crossword puzzle

Across: 1 James' new name: Mr G. ?, 5 opposite of 'exception', 6 he is used ? taking a siesta, 7 the fishing rod for the ? arm, 8 opposite of 'multi', 11 Spain is on the ? Peninsula, 12 ? the Basques! 15 Pedro's hotels are there, 16 opposite of 'hero', 17 put (on the market), 18 insult; call someone names,

Down: 1 it's not a real island, 2 SASL sell aids for ? learners, 3 English for 'Eindringling', 4 James' new first name, 5 angling equipment, 8 James' surfboards have got it, 9 Spanish for 'sleep', 10 the Spanish are ?-tasking, 13 problems are ? to arise, 14 typical Spanish male person

Chapter 10

FOCUS ON FRANCE
Splitting hairs in Strasbourg

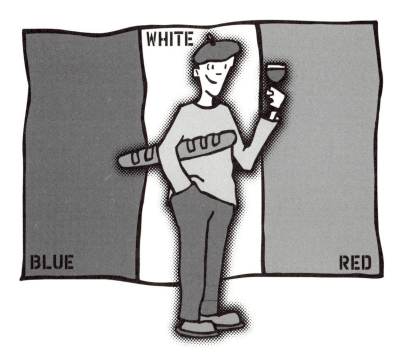

☺ Time for a smile

French politicians say: "We want Britain to take her proper place in Europe" ... and they mean, "... somewhere behind Albania or Lithuania."

When General de Gaulle died, Noël Coward was asked what he thought the General and God would find to talk about in Heaven. Coward replied, "That depends on how good God's French is."

Chapter 10

🎧 Splitting hairs in Strasbourg

James arrives in Strasbourg in the border region in the east of France. The Alsace is an area of mixed French and German language and culture. He stays at a small hotel in Strasbourg itself.

> The meeting with T.C.L (Tennis Club Loisirs) takes place on a hot day in June at 9 o'clock in the morning. James Kelly (**J**), Mr Kratzenberg (**K**), Mr Gordois (**G**), Mrs Schleicher (**S**)

(Sound of knocking at the door. James enters. He is wearing an Hawaiian shirt and light brown casual trousers. No tie, no jacket.)

K: Je suis désolé, Monsieur, mais vous vous êtes trompé de porte sans doute.

J: My name is Kelly, James Kelly.

K: Ah ... Monsieur Kelly (*He looks him up and down*) ... excusez-moi ... we've been expecting you. Has anything gone wrong?

J: Not at all. Why do you ask?

All: (*Mumbling*)

K: It's my great pleasure, lady and gentlemen, to introduce the representative of SASL to you. Since Mr Kelly hasn't been able to bring his interpreter, we'll have to conduct the meeting in English for a change. I hope, Mr Kelly, you'll forgive our pronunciation. Mr Kelly, may I present our little team to you? My name's Kratzenberg. I'm the president of this establishment. On my right is Mr Gordois, our director of sport, and to his right you see Mrs Schleicher, my assistant. She will take the minutes of this meeting for later reference ...
(James looks at the three. They are indeed all dressed in an extremely formal manner. Both gentlemen are wearing dark suits and the lady has a blue costume on. James feels out of place somehow.)

K: (*continues*) And now, gentlemen, if you are ready I'd like to declare this meeting open. Mr Gordois will give us a resumé of the situation up to now?

G: Certainly, sir. Mr Kelly, your company sent us detailed documentation on your product Tennis Systems for the Untalented, the T.S.U., version 1.3, as you call it. For our part we gave you a report on the

FOCUS ON FRANCE 10

size of our operation, the number of training centres we own or manage. You know we are the market leader. And we furnished you with our rough estimates for such lazy learner systems.

J: Excuse me, not lazy learners. Systems for the untalented. It sounds more positive.

G: I'm sorry, Mr Kelly, but for our French ear 'lazy' is a more friendly word than 'untalented'.

J: Oh, you mean you've more lazy people here in France than untalented ones. It's the same everywhere.

K: I'm sure, Mr Kelly, that France has no more and no fewer lazy or untalented people than any other ... hm ... civilised country. Has anybody a term that is both neutral and precise?

S: What about the 'less talented learner'?

K: Thank-you for your contribution, Mrs Schleicher, but what's the difference between 'untalented' and 'less talented'? Mr Gordois, you are our linguist. Would you like to comment on this?

G: Well, if you ask me, I'd call it a SHE: La Solution Humaine pour l'Erudit ('the humane solution for the scholar') since the academic is – present company excepted – more at home in the lofty heights of philosophy and so by nature less devoted to and consequently less dextrous in the plains of matters physical or, as Descartes would have put it, Cogi ...

J: Excuse me gents, but I didn't understand a word of what you were saying. And I don't care whether you call it SHE, HE, IT or whatever Mr Descartes pleases to call our rackets, as long as he is ready to take a few hundred.

K: Mr Gordois, I think we should put the linguistic question on the agenda of our next staff meeting where we will have to find a French brandname for the thing. Perhaps you could continue now.

G: Certainly, sir. As I was saying, we have given your company our approximate requirements. We know the cost to ourselves and because of the size of the initial order we expect, of course, the appropriate discount.

J: Well, the cost per tennis training system in total comes to 200 dollars. If we ...

Chapter 10

K: I beg your pardon, Mr Kelly, but in your documentation you quoted us a figure of 150 dollars per system. Surely you did not get your figures wrong?

J: Yes, we did talk about 150 dollars for the version 1.1. but we implemented some improvements to the racket and system. If I could explain we ... *(fade out)*.

... *(fade in)* And so with the adaptable size, the variable stringing system, the beeper or alternatively the vibrator built into the handle we believe you have good value for money.

K: That's very interesting but it's almost twelve o'clock midday. Time to enjoy some of our French cuisine. We will continue with our discussions after the meal.

J: Sounds great to me. Say, I was walking in the city yesterday evening. Everyone seemed to be speaking German. And the food was very similar to the stuff I ate in Germany a couple of weeks ago.

K: Similar but not the same. The language here is a dialect of French and here we have Alsatian specialities.

J: It seems that they were speaking more German than French and the food was mainly pork and sauerkraut.

K: Alsatian, not German. Ah, my young friend, what does an American know of le savoir-vivre, the fine art of living? Allons-y!

J: I might not understand European culture, but I'm not deaf and blind.

(M) Mind your manners

What you should not say to a Frenchman.
- → I'd rather have a bottle of Californian red.
- → What did your father do during the German occupation?
- → Alsatia is not much different from Germany.
- → What's the French for 'arrogant chauvinist'?

☺ Time for a smile

They say when you go to France you should spend some time at the Folies Bergères, but this isn't easy when you've only two weeks' holiday.

FOCUS ON FRANCE 10

B Task 1: Train your brain

More than one answer might be correct.

1. What is the meeting about?
   - a James is presenting the T.S.U.
   - b Tennis Club Loisir are going to place an order for the T.S.U.
   - c They are discussing the quotation of SASL

2. What is a T.S.U.?
   - a It is a collapsible golf club.
   - b It is a racket that gives acoustic and tactile signals to correct the body position and the swing of the player.
   - c The Tennis Systems for the Untalented is a robotised trainer.

3. Why do they disagree about the price?
   - a SASL's quotation and James' price per unit do not correspond.
   - b The new improved version 1.3 is more expensive.
   - c James got his figures wrong.

L Watch their Ways: Meetings à la française

1. Appointments should be prepared in writing. Business letters should be written in correct business French otherwise they will be ignored.
2. The French are almost always late for a meeting. Being on time means "being within 15 minutes of the appointed hour." However, they expect foreigners to be punctual.
3. Meetings are formal occasions. They expect you to be dressed appropriately. Jackets and ties are not taken off during meetings.
4. Participants are introduced according to their ranks.
5. Meetings are conducted in French. If you don't speak it fluently you had better bring a colleague who has mastered the language or forget about the deal.
6. They come to the meeting well-prepared. They don't like changes to previously agreed terms.
7. They are fighting hard to preserve their language. English or American terms must be translated into French (oil-rig : un appareil de forage en mer; walkman : un baladeur; hitparade : le palmarès).

Chapter 10

8. The French see themselves as the only truly civilised people in the world. They believe they are intellectually superior to any other nationality.
9. The French examine everything through a philosophical microscope. They regard it as an intellectual exercise. That is why meetings can be long and wordy.

B Task 2: Cross-cultural awareness test

Have a second look at the meeting. Then try to put the correct numbers from the above list (page 127 f.) next to the quotation.

Mon dieu! Monsieur Kelly, has anything gone wrong?	3
.. or, as Descartes would have put it, Cogi ...	
Since Mr Kelly hasn't been able to bring his interpreter, we'll have to conduct the meeting in English for a change.	
Monsieur Kelly, we've been expecting you.	
My name's Kratzenberg. I'm the president of this establishment. On my right is Mr Gordois, our director of sport, and to his right you see Mrs Schleicher, my assistant.	
Ah, my young friend, what does an American know of le savoir-vivre?	
I'm sure, Mr Kelly, that France has no more and no fewer lazy or untalented people than any other ... hm ... civilised country.	
I beg your pardon, Mr Kelly, but in your documentation you quoted us a figure of 155 dollars per system.	
I think we should put the linguistic question on the agenda of our next staff meeting where we will have to find a French brandname for the thing.	

☺ Time for a grin: James Kelly's diary

Have you ever eaten in a Paris restaurant?
The real waiters[1] are the customers.

---

1 Kellner; Wartender

FOCUS ON FRANCE 10

B Task 3: Patchwork – Words chairmen will use

comment		resumé		declare
	conduct		agenda	
present		contribution		reference
	continue		pleasure	

Can you put the patches in their right places?

It's my great .... to introduce Mr James Kelly to you.

Mr Kelly, may I .... our little team to you?

We'll have to .... the meeting in English for a change.

And now I'd like to .... this meeting open.

My assistant will take the minutes of this meeting for later ....

Mr Gordois will give us a .... of the situation up to now.

Mr Gordois, would you like to .... on this?

I think we should put the linguistic question on the ....

of our next staff meeting.

Thank-you for your .... , Mrs Schleicher.

We will .... with our discussions after the meal.

☺ How the French are seen by others

They are not really admired by anyone except the Italians. Other Europeans find them conservative, chauvinistic, brilliant, superficial and not very friendly.

Guide to National Practices in Western Europe.
Parkland Research Europe

B Task 4: Understanding more American English

Yanks and Brits are often at cross-purposes even when they mean the same thing. Can you match time and places? It is confusing, isn't it?

	British English		American English
1.	We've bought the *block of flats*.	a	I thought it was on the first *floor*.
2.	It's at the big *crossroads*.	b	We expect you *4/12/1998*.
3.	Paul's office is on the *first floor*.	c	I thought it was at an *intersection*.
4.	My office is on the *ground floor*.	d	The *12/4/1998* will be too early.
5.	I'll arrive on *12/4/1998*.	e	I'd have preferred an *apartment house*.
6.	The *4/12/1998* will be fine.	f	And I thought your office was on the *second floor*.

☺ How the French see other nations

The Germans: They no longer hate the Germans, but they aren't fond of them. They feel culturally and politically superior to them and are afraid of their industrial power.

The English: They see them as small-minded, uncultured, dressing and eating badly, and spending most of their time gardening, playing cricket and drinking sweet, warm beer instead of Champagne. To the French, the evacuation of the British forces from Dunkirk in 1940 was a cowardly act. That is why they find the English untrustworthy.

The Belgians: The French have nothing but contempt for the Belgians. They are the target of countless French jokes. "Why have the Arabs all the oil and the Belgians all the potatoes?" – "When God distributed the wealth of the earth he offered the Belgians the first choice."

Nick Yapp and Michael Syrett

FOCUS ON FRANCE 10

☺ Letter from France

Dear Dave,

I'm not so sure things are going well for me here in France. Portugal was great, though. We'll have to do a vacation there. They have great beaches there just like in the movies. France is different though. They're so formal. Jesus, I felt right out of place in the meeting yesterday. They were all dressed up as if they were going to a funeral.
And they didn't stop talking and pontificating. They seemed more interested in splitting linguistic hairs than in the business itself. They would arrange for everything to be translated into French professionally and we should pay. I tried to explain that it should be in English since customers would come from all over Europe and English was the language of international communication. The CEO nearly blew his top telling me French was the international language of diplomacy. Wow!
We didn't hit it off about food either. He just didn't want to accept that it was the same as in Germany. They only pronounce it different – the sauerkraut of the French, or whatever it is there. They say something like "shukrut". Arrogant bunch!

Yours Jamie

PS. They didn't even come to a decision about the equipment. What's the point of a meeting without decisions? See you in a couple of weeks. I'm flying to Russia tomorrow. I don't know if I'm looking forward to that.

☺ Time for a grin: James Kelly's diary

It's hard to describe a French waiter.
Picture[1] a New York cab driver with an apron[2].

---

1 sich vorstellen 2 Schürze

Chapter 10

B Task 5: The travelling manager's country quiz

1. Let's suppose you want to build a factory for which you need a large site. Let's suppose further that your product is a bit dangerous for the environment. Which European country would you go for?

   a France
   b Germany
   c Netherlands

2. If you want to break into a foreign market, population is one factor you have to take into consideration. Which three countries have the same number of inhabitants?

   a Denmark
   b Belgium
   c Ireland
   d Netherlands
   e Portugal
   f Spain

3. You are preparing your presentations in several European countries. In which country is it not advisable to sprinkle your talk with jokes and humorous quotations?

   a France
   b Belgium
   c Switzerland

4. In which country is it most difficult for James to settle disagreement by compromise?

   a France
   b Portugal
   c Germany

5. James wants to advertise his T.S.U on French television. How much is VAT on advertising in the French media?

   a 20.6 %
   b 18.6 %
   c 16.6 %

6. James intends to visit the following companies. Write the country next to the company. Can you help him?

	Company	Country
Eurosports	(BV)	....
Topgolf	(SpA)	....
Unisports	(SA)	....
Allrounders	(Lda)	....

FOCUS ON FRANCE 10

(L) Going international: Business in France is a serious matter

Meetings will follow an established format with a detailed agenda. There will be no small talk, which is so typical of the American or British sales pitch. Neither is humour used to break the ice or to warm up the audience. So do not sprinkle your presentation with jokes, because business is a serious matter. Like Mr Gordois, participants come well prepared for the contribution they are expected to make.

In England or Germany managers come from the population at large. The French senior executive is drawn from the elite educational institutions. He is highly-educated, self-assured and usually the best speaker at the meeting. He will not be seriously contradicted. To question his ideas is to question his authority and competence.

The French see the meeting as a social occasion and a forum for their own cleverness. Cold logic leads to the right conclusion. They want to be precise at all times. That is why they refuse to make concessions or to compromise. They enjoy a good rational argument on an impersonal intellectual level and disagree for the sake of discussion. Often they end up with a totally new problem and discuss it with great satisfaction.

Business after working hours is part of the job. They honour guests at the best restaurants with three to six-course meals. The American who talks business to a Frenchman over dinner will find his French colleague wants to enjoy his meal. French people believe that there is more to life than the job. Eating is part of the secret of good life. They do not admire workaholics, so don't talk business over lunch.

Avoid conversation openers that are popular in England, Germany and the States: ("What do you do for a living?", "Are you married?", "Do you have children?"). Keep to the Tour de France, their excellent food or discuss art and culture, if you can master the subjects. If not, you can score points by criticising the English – a favourite French pastime.

☺ Time for a smile

I have not always in my dealings with Charles de Gaulle found quotations from Trafalgar and Waterloo necessarily productive, and he has been very tactful about the Battle of Hastings.

Harold Wilson, 1967

10 Chapter

(V) Vocabulary to help you with the text

academic	Akademiker
admire	bewundern
Alsatian specialities	elsässische Spezialitäten
appropriate	angemessen
approximate requirements	ungefähre Anforderungen
blow one's top	die Beherrschung verlieren
border region	Grenzgebiet
brandname	Markenname
casual trousers	lässige Hosen, Freizeithosen
conclusion	Schlußfolgerung
conduct the meeting	eine Besprechung führen, leiten
contempt	Verachtung
continue	fortfahren
correspond	entsprechen
cowardly act	feige Handlung
cross-purposes; be at ~	aneinander vorbeireden
devoted; be ~ to	sich widmen, hingeben
dextrous	geschickt, fingerfertig
diplomacy	Diplomatie
distribute	verteilen
drop a bombshell	eine Bombe platzen lassen
environment	Umwelt
establishment	Firma, Unternehmen
estimate; rough ~	grobe Schätzung
feel out of place	sich deplaziert fühlen
first floor (AE)	Erdgeschoß (USA)
for our part	was uns betrifft
funeral	Beerdigung
furnish someone with	jemanden beliefern, versorgen mit
good value for money	preiswert
handle	Griff
hit it off with	sich gut verstehen mit
honour (v.)	ehren
implement improvements	Verbesserungen einbauen
initial order	erster Auftrag

FOCUS ON FRANCE 10

interpreter	Dolmetscher
intersection (AE)	Kreuzung (USA)
l'érudit (franz.)	Gelehrter
lazy	faul
lofty heights	erhabene Höhen
loisirs (franz.)	Freizeit
market leader	Marktführer
master the language	die Sprache beherrschen
matters; physical ~	materielle Dinge
mumbling	Gemurmel
occupation	hier: Besatzung
operation	Unternehmen; Firma
pontificate	dogmatisch sein; predigen
present company excepted	Anwesende ausgenommen
preserve the language	die Sprache bewahren
previously agreed terms	zuvor vereinbarte Bedingungen
proprietor	Eigentümer
quotation	Angebot; Zitat
quote	hier: ein Angebot machen
reference; for later ~	hier: für späteren Gebrauch
requirements	Anforderungen, Bedürfnisse
sake; for the ~ of discussion	um der Diskussion willen
scholar	Gelehrter
scholarly learner	akademischer Schüler
score points	Punkte sammeln
self-assured	selbstsicher
similar	ähnlich
site	Gelände, Grundstück
size	Umfang, Größe
social occasion	gesellschaftliches Ereignis
split hairs	Haare spalten
stringing system	Bespannung (des Schlägers)
superficial	oberflächlich
superior; be ~ to someone	jemandem überlegen sein
tactile	tastbar, fühlbar
tie	Krawatte
untrustworthy	unzuverlässig

Chapter 10

up to now	bis jetzt, soweit
VAT (value added tax)	Mehrwertsteuer
vous vous êtes trompé de porte	Sie haben sich in der Tür geirrt

☺ Hit them on the head

Paris is a disease[1]; sometimes it is several diseases.

Honoré de Balzac

The French complain[2] about everything and always.

Napoléon Bonaparte

The French will only be united under the threat[3] of danger.
Nobody can bring together a country that has 256 kinds of cheese.

Charles de Gaulle, 1951

The only country where the money falls apart[4]
 and you can't tear the toilet paper.

Billy Wilder

---

1 Krankheit 2 sich beschweren 3 Bedrohung 4 zerfallen

Chapter 11

FOCUS ON RUSSIA
Building bridges in Moscow

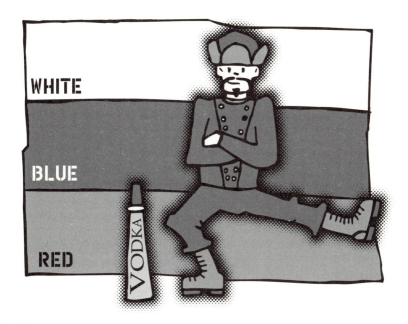

🙂 Time for a smile

Ivan opened a fish restaurant and the business was good. Boris heard about it and stopped by.
"It's good to see you, Ivan. Can you lend me ten rubles?"
"I'd like to, but I really can't," sighed[1] Ivan. "You see, I've signed a contract with the bank next door. They are not going to sell fish, and I'm not going to lend money."

---

1 seufzen

11 Chapter

🎧 Building bridges in Moscow

> James Kelly is on flight 604 to Moscow. He is travelling with Aeroflot, the state airline. It's a pretty rough flight and the service leaves a lot to be desired. James (**J**) is sitting next to a well-travelled compatriot Sam Hodges (**S**).

J: Man, what a scraggy-looking piece of chicken. I sure hope things will get better when we're inside Russia.

S: I'm very much afraid they won't, son. They're suffering from a shortage of most everything in that country, specially since the arrival of capitalism.

J: Gee, I'd have thought things would have gotten better with the introduction of supply and demand.

S: Not in the least. You can't just switch from state enterprises to lean market-oriented companies over night. It'll take decades.

J: Never given it much thought but I guess you're right. Say, you seem to know a lot about Russia. You got business there?

S: You bet! Sam Hodges is my name. I'm a co-ordinator for a big aid project that we're implementing in Russia. Been living in Moscow for more than two years.

J: Wow! Jamie, James Kelly. I'm doing some negotiations for our company. We sell sports equipment to sports centres in various countries.

S: That figures. There are a lot of leisure facilities springing up everywhere. Be careful, though. You won't just be discussing with CEOs. Either the government or some sort of Mafia will be in the background.

J: Jesus!

S: Don't sweat it! No big deal. It just means they won't make any final decisions at a meeting. You'll have to keep coming back.

J: Say Sam, could you give me some advice on how to deal with these Russians, from your experience I mean?

S: Sure can. You can't unlock a door with the wrong key, and you will have a hard time getting started abroad if you see the wrong people. Find the decision-maker!

J: That's easier said than done.

S: Our organisation even has guidelines on it. Here you are!

J: Wow! You sure have done your homework.

FOCUS ON RUSSIA

S: Well, we've learned the hard way. What was I going to say ... the decision-maker? He – and it's always a 'he' in Russia – might be the most senior member in their team – an old expert or veteran.

J: I suppose I won't be dealing with men of my own age then.

S: Maybe you will. But there'll sure as hell be an old fox. And in the negotiation they'll always be thinking several moves ahead, like in chess.

J: And what about the style of the discussions?

S: Russians can talk tough, and with one voice. They work as a group. So don't try to split them. And they don't generally like to compromise. If you try to meet them halfway they'll regard it as a sign of weakness.

J: Gee, sounds like a hard nut to crack.

S: But there are ways to get the upper hand. And they don't feel comfortable if you drop new proposals and ideas all over the place. They are a conservative, nostalgic bunch and there have been more dramatic changes recently than they seem to be able to swallow.

J: Is there anything special to watch out for!

S: Yeah, for example, your partners here may bring an initial draft outlining their position to the first meeting. Don't be fooled by it! Don't give in too easily. It's not their final position. And they may certainly have some built-in throwaways, as we call them. They make concessions on some minor matters to get bigger concessions from you.

J: This is beginning to sound daunting.

S: And they'll expect you to start off the negotiation. That gives them time to study you. Finally, beware of contracts. A signature on a piece of paper is not as binding in Moscow as it is in Washington. They're made of "rubber" in the eyes of the Russians. They stick to them as long as things are going well and they can profit by them. They'll bend 'em as soon as things go wrong.

J: Well, thank you, sir, for that information. It sounds like damn hard work.

S: That was the bad news. The good news is the Russians are very people-oriented, not deal-oriented. Strict rules are out. So you have to break the ice, get personal and open up to them. They are interested in your hopes, emotions and personal goals.

11 Chapter

J: And what's the best way to do that?

S: Vodka, Jamie, vodka.

J: Oh my God! More alcohol, just like in Ireland.

S: Exactly. There's a similarity between Irish and Russians. They like to drink, but it's social drinking. Make it clear to them, that you're happy to sit down and drink good Russian vodka with them and you're in! They prefer to drink sitting, you know. Also be careful in general when you check if they've understood something. They always say they've understood even if they haven't. But take that drinking seriously – it's bridge-building. Even drinking between meals.

J: Wow! What sort of people are they?

S: They like to search their souls and they love conversation. They don't like authorities so you can criticise your own. They'll understand that. But most important – build those bridges.

J: Bridges? Which bridges?

S: Open up your heart, soul or whatever you think that's special about your person. They are interested in your hopes, in your family. Show them photos of Mom, Dad and the little ones. Do business in saunas and in restaurants.

J: Well, thanks for the advice, Sam. I'll see what I can do.

> In a hotel in Moscow. In the middle of the afternoon in the middle of James Kelly's (**J**) negotiations with Boris Zhukov (**B**), Leo Stravinsky (**L**) and Yury Plokov (**P**).

(fade in, sounds of laughing)

B: Gentlemen, this is all very interesting but I'm beginning to feel a little thirsty. Shall we break for a lemon tea?

J: That'd be great! But I've also heard that your Russian vodka is the best in the world at any time.

B: Indeed our 'little water' is very special. This is a suggestion I feel we cannot refuse. It is a real joy to share part of our culture with a visitor. Leo, can you arrange everything?

L: Naturally, and I believe vodka will help us to connect even better with our young American friend.

J: Sounds like a good plan to me.

B: *(whispering to Leo)* Strange coincidence! Doesn't this boy remind you of that James Kelly we met in Hollerberg?

FOCUS ON RUSSIA

Task 1: Train your brain

What can we learn from the conversation on the plane?

1. Why does Sam compare Russian negotiators with chess players?
2. What does it really mean when Russians make minor concessions?
3. "They don't feel comfortable if you drop new proposals and ideas all over the place," says Sam. Can you imagine why?
4. Sam advises James not to compromise. Why?
5. What do you do when they present you with a draft of a contract?
6. Why does Sam recommend James to beware of contracts?
7. Russians are people-orientated. That's why Sam advises James to build bridges. Name three ways of doing this.

Task 2: Understanding American English

**Look at the text. Here are the British English Expressions.
What did James or Sam say?**

British English	American English
What a thin-looking piece of chicken!	....
I thought things had improved.	....
You can be sure about that.	....
Don't get nervous!	....
I certainly can.	....
It's nothing special.	....

☺ Time for a smile: Marketing in Russia

Marketing in our place is carefully planned. Every time there is a shortage[1] of bacon, there's a shortage in eggs.

---

1 Knappheit, Mangel

(M) Watch their ways: How to build bridges

1. They are people-orientated rather than deal-orientated. They are interested in your hopes, emotions and personal goals. They are fond of soul-searching.
2. They love children more than most of us: exchanging of photographs is an excellent way to build bridges.
3. They prefer to drink sitting down with time to make frequent speeches and toasts.
4. When they touch another person during conversation it is a sign of confidence.
5. Business is also done in the sauna and in the restaurant.

(B) Task 3: True (T) or false (F)

Are you ready to do business in Russia? Test yourself.   T   F

1. They use tough talk if they feel in a stronger position.
2. Bluntness wins friends both in Detroit and in Kiev.
3. Keep smiling when getting to know them in meetings.
4. A contract is binding as long as both sides profit from it.
5. Personal relationships are more important than money.
6. Russians are not title and status-conscious.
7. They negotiate step by step, like Germans and Americans.
8. Excessive profit margins are looked on as illegitimate.

☺ Time for a smile

A Russian official visited a car factory. The director showed him around and at the end of the tour offered him a free car to be delivered within three months. "Oh no," sighed the official, "I cannot accept it." – "Well then, we'll sell it to you for ten rubles." The official handed him twenty rubles and said, "In that case I'll have two."

FOCUS ON RUSSIA

B Task 4: How do different nations view contracts?

Put the right numbers next to the statements:
France 1; Italy 2; Portugal 3; Japan 4; Russia 5.

A contract is binding and must be fulfilled. ☐

A contract is a statement of intent and will be reworked when necessary. ☐

A contract that is fulfilled six months later than agreed is better than no contract at all. ☐

A contract is binding as long as both sides profit by it. ☐

L Letter from Russia

Hi Dave,

Sorry I couldn't E-mail you. No computer, no line to the outside. I've had a great time here in Russia. I would never have believed it. I got some good advice from an American citizen on the plane. And somehow he was right. He said I should get real personal with them and drink vodka. Well, I did it and I liked it. I'm not sure I got a lot of business done but I got on excellently with Boris, Leo and Yury. They're fine guys, almost like Americans, but with a Russian accent and a hankering for vodka.

There's not much to eat around here in restaurants but the good thing is that privately the people share everything with you. I guess you've just got to build bridges to them, as some people would say. You know I think somehow the Russians have had a bad press. Anyhow in a couple of days I'm flying to Saudi Arabia according to our schedule. I know you know but I just wanted to remind you.

Regards,
James

Chapter 11

B Task 5: The travelling manager's country quiz

More than one answer might be correct.

1. Like Americans, the Russians think big. The Russian Federation is
   - **a** twice as big as the United States
   - **b** 30 times bigger than France
   - **c** 20 times bigger than Germany
2. The travelling manager should know how many time zones the Russian Federation covers.

   a 4   **b** 7   **c** 11
3. Population figures are important if you want to invest in a new market.
   - **a** With 150 million people, Russia has less than half of the population of the European Union.
   - **b** In its 20 republics and 55 regions more people live than in the United States.
   - **c** Russia has as many inhabitants as Portugal, France and Spain together.
4. Where and how do your future customers live? The distribution of the population over a country decides where you target your advertising campaign.
   - **a** Russia's population is evenly spread all over the country.
   - **b** 75 per cent of the population live in cities.
   - **c** More than a third of the population live in cities of more than half a million people.
5. How many of the formerly state-owned businesses have been privatised?

   a 75%   **b** 5 %   **c** 35%
6. One tends to forget that Russia was communist only for a very short period whereas Russians have been Orthodox Christians for more than a thousand years. How long was Russia communist?
   - **a** about 150 years
   - **b** about 100 years
   - **c** about 80 years

(L) Going international: Doing business with Russians

It is not easy to do business in Russia, especially with ministries because there is still a lot of red tape to overcome before a contract is signed.

How to open the door. You can't unlock a door with the wrong key and you will have a hard time getting started abroad if you see the wrong people. Find the decision-maker! Spending time with subordinates, however qualified, is a waste of time. That is why you should send a high-level manager rather than a highly qualified but low-level specialist. Russians are status-conscious. Sending low status representatives will be understood as a lack of respect. The visitor must be high enough in the hierarchy to reach a decision-maker.

Meetings and greetings. Shake hands when first meeting people and upon leaving. Introductions are informal and direct. A smile is only used as a greeting among personal friends. Smiling is not respectful on formal occasions and smiling for no reason is a sign of idiocy. Russians are still very title-conscious: use titles and show respect. Russians think of themselves as being absolutely honest and trustworthy. So don't show distrust. Like most nations they are proud of their country. Don't tell them that in your country everything is bigger, cleaner and better organised.

Negotiating contracts. Russians are searching for their Slavic soul. That is why others sometimes find their Russian partners sentimental and gloomy. However, they are almost always well-trained negotiators and specialists in their field who plan and prepare carefully. Presentations should be full of technical detail. They negotiate as a team and speak with one voice, unlike Italians or Americans. So don't try to split them up or play them off against each other. When American participants speak with several voices or argue among themselves they may be confused about who has the real authority. Remember: No agreement is final until it is signed.

11 Chapter

Entertainment. Dinner is eaten early. If you are invited to a Russian home, it is customary to bring flowers, vodka or wine. Dinner is eaten at about six o'clock or whenever they feel hungry. Toasts are common, and the guest must be prepared to return toasts. Among younger businessmen you will find more and more non-smokers, teetotallers and even vegetarians. Invitations could include a ballet, circus, concert or dinner in a restaurant.

Vocabulary to help you with the text

advice	Rat
build bridges	Brücken bauen
coincidence	Zufall
crack; hard nut to ~	eine harte Nuß knacken
customary	üblich
daunting; sound ~	entmutigend klingen
decade; it'll take ~s	das dauert Jahrzehnte
decision-maker	Entscheidungsträger
distribution of the population	Verteilung der Bevölkerung
drop new ideas all over the place	mit neuen Ideen um sich werfen
fox; an old ~	ein alter Fuchs
guidelines	Richtlinien
hankering for vodka	Hang zum, Vorliebe für Wodka
have a bad press	keinen guten Ruf haben
idiocy	Irrsinn, Torheit
initial draft	erster Entwurf
intent	Absicht
lack of respect	Respektlosigkeit
lean companies	verschlankte Firmen
leisure facilities	Freizeiteinrichtungen
meet someone halfway	jemandem auf halbem Wege entgegenkommen
move; think several ~s ahead	mehrere Züge vorausdenken

FOCUS ON RUSSIA

negotiation	Verhandlung
no big deal	nichts Besonderes
be on top of the situation	über der Situation stehen
outline a position	eine Position umreißen
personal goals	persönliche Ziele
proposal	Vorschlag
red tape	Bürokratie
refuse a suggestion	einen Vorschlag ablehnen
return toasts	Trinksprüche erwidern
scraggy	mager, dürr
search one's soul	seine Seele erforschen
sign of confidence	Zeichen des Vertrauens
status-conscious	statusbewußt
stick to	sich halten an
subordinate	Untergebener
supply and demand	Angebot und Nachfrage
swallow	schlucken
talk tough	zäh verhandeln
target a campaign	eine Kampagne ausrichten auf
teetotaller	Abstinenzler
throwaways	hier: Scheinforderungen, Scheinbedingungen

☺ Food for thought

Russians are puzzled that westerners can spend the equivalent of a Russian's annual salary in Moscow hotels and restaurants, but balk[1] at giving them a fax machine so that they can communicate more easily.

John Mole, *Mind Your Manners*

---

1 zurückscheuen vor

11 Chapter

B A crossword puzzle to test the vocabulary

Across: 2 steaks and talks can be ?, 5 Russian contracts are like it, 6 ten years, 7 he has a hankering ? vodka, 8 Russians have a deep Slavic ?, 11 Russia isn't a republic but a ?, 13 Russians have had a bad ?, 16 repair the verb: Tegart, 17 in Russia you should ? bridges, 18 an old fox or soldier

Down: 1 let's meet them ?, 3 another word for target (n.), 4 you must ? their toasts, 5 bureaucracy means ? tape, 6 English for 'Entwurf', 9 Sam gave James some good ?, 10 some nuts are hard to ?, 12 be on ? of the situation, 14 divide a group, 15 red ?

148

FOCUS ON SAUDI ARABIA
Balls and clubs for combat

Chapter 12

☺ Time for a smile

"Any alcohol?" demanded the Saudi customs official. "No, thanks," answered Klaus, "I've got enough of it in my suitcase."

Chapter 12

Fax from America

Hi Jamie,

How's life at your end? I've just started my new job at your sports company. So we'll be able to see more of each other. It must be hot and sandy out there in the Middle East. Speaking of that I've got all that information on how to behave in Arab countries. It was a lot so I've summarized it for you.

1. First, don't say anything to insult their country. They believe they were world leaders and can be again. Of course we just see them living off oil revenues. Don't say anything like that to them.

2. Here in the West we are individual-oriented. They are centered on the family. So if you get the chance, wish members of the family the best. But not any of the females — don't compliment on cooking. Take the women's work for granted, or you'll be up to your neck in it.

3. On the theme of modernizing. We want to modernize, but they'll prefer to preserve their traditions. Don't be too pushy!

5. You have to convince them that you're an honest trader. Don't talk logic. Talk feelings.

6. For goodness sake, don't play the strong and dominant American theme. The Arabs like to support and respect the weak.

7. When you meet Arabs, they will tend to talk a lot about family and connections. For God's sake don't stop them and suggest getting back to business. Don't be impatient like you so often are. Remember everything in Arab countries is a matter of personal relationships.

9. There's a point I don't really need to mention to you, distance! Arabs tend to come very close to you when speaking. They touch a lot

FOCUS ON SAUDI ARABIA 12

> as well. Don't move away, if possible, otherwise they'll feel you're being arrogant.
>
> 10. Don't worry or get angry if they don't arrive exactly on time. And remember, Jamie. No alcohol (you'll find that a bit of a shock after Russia), no improper dress, no criticizing Islam.
>
> 11. Look them in the eye when talking to them. They depend a lot on eye contact. And try praising their country, art, dress and food (but not their women).
>
> I'm looking forward to seeing you soon.
>
> Love, Jane
>
> P.S. Dave (you remember, our boss) said he's going to surprise you. He'll be arriving in Saudi to help with the discussions.

True pitfalls for managers

Case 1

A major American company built a hospital in Saudi Arabia, bringing the best of modern American medicine to the desert. The Arabs did not like it. They were offended by the cool and impersonal efficiency of the doctors, the unfamiliar meals, the incomprehensible 'starvation' of patients before surgery and the 'inhumane' exclusion of relatives from isolation areas. The administrator, a highly competent executive by American standards ... returned to the United States before his assignment was complete.

Case 2

Singer had to revise its advertising campaign in the Middle East when it learned that not the women, but the husbands were the buyers and they were not interested in saving their wives' personal effort. Singer had to convince Arab men that sewing machines would make their wives more useful and better able to attend to their husbands' needs.

Source: Lennie Copeland, Lewis Griggs, *Going International*

Chapter 12

🎧 Two Americans in Saudi Arabia

James Kelly (**J**), our hero and Dave (**D**), his older boss, are discussing their imminent meeting with Mr Ibn Ben Saadi, who is responsible for many recreation facilities in Saudi Arabia.

J: Well, I'd sure like to thank you for all the confidence you've placed in me. It isn't every day that you get a chance to visit places like Russia and Saudi Arabia.

D: And that's why I'm here, too. You know, Jamie, it's always been our policy at SASL to help our junior management to develop themselves further. You should all learn to take responsibility for the company. I absolutely support this strategy. Normally I don't have time to go abroad myself. Young managers should be entrusted with ... anyway, you know what I mean, don't you?

J: That's very kind of you to say so, Dave. By the way, I've been preparing some background stuff on etiquette and behaviour in Saudi.

D: Don't waste your time! We don't have a company psychologist and I know why. Know your products! That's all you're required to do and contracts will take care of themselves. In the discussion just concentrate on our sales arguments. Just wait for an opening and jump in. American style. Bang – and you've landed the contract. Don't worry about all this cultural fuzz.

J: With due respect, Dave, I've picked up a lot of tips in Europe on how to manage in different countries. I ...

D: Now, now. None of this theoretical nonsense! Do I get hot about these things?

J: Well, I have quite a relaxed thing going on with our Saudi customer.

D: Right, and I'm here to make it even smoother. When have we got the meeting? At two o'clock? See you then.

Hours later; no contract has been signed. Dave is getting impatient.
Dave Makeit (**D**), James Kelly (**J**), Ibn Ben Saadi (**S**)

D: I must apologise for joining you so late, Your Excellency. I just couldn't leave you the whole time in the hands of junior manage-

FOCUS ON SAUDI ARABIA

ment. So I've come to your lovely country by the Persian Gulf. And I've brought Mrs Rubinstein, our specialist in Mohammedan law. She'll help us to finalize the contract.

S: I see. If you couldn't leave me in the hands of a junior, then why did you do it?

D: Hmm! ... It was a question of time ...

S: Was it? Well, your junior and myself have had a very constructive discussion. We've even got as far as exchanging our opinions about horse races, a pastime we both have in common.

D: James, have you been talking about animals? Well, I simply have to apologise to you Mr Saadi that Mr Kelly has been wasting your time talking about horses.

J: Dave, it's a personal interest of His Excellency. I thought ...

D: You aren't paid to think ... you're paid to sell our special clubs for sandy golf courses in desert countries.

S: Well, we've some very nice grass courses here in Saudi, too. I have the turf brought here from Britain twice a year.

J: That's right, Dave. Mr Saadi isn't very interested in our clubs but I think we've hit the bullseye with the "beeping" golfball for the officers that are stationed along the borders. They seem to lose hundreds of balls in the sand dunes, especially when there is a strong wind blowing, you see.

D: No clubs then! I see. Hmm ... By the way, did you mention the bikes?

S: What do you mean, sir, bikes?

D: Bicycles. Desert bikes! Another great idea! A special bike which we have produced, just for you people in the desert. It's just what you folks need in this part of the world. *(He opens a catalogue)* Here you are: the robust model for the nomad, a smaller one for the children and our deluxe model for women, with an extra broad saddle. It has special gears that are easy on their delicate legs.

S: Mister Dave, I think we don't need things easy on our legs. We have our camels and our Cadillacs. Excuse me, Gentlemen, I feel we must bring this discussion to an end ... *(to Dave)* Thank you for having given me so much of your valuable time ... but I've promised to show our young friend our stables. Since you don't seem to like horses and camels I suggest that you try one of my Cadillacs. My chauffeur will show you the sights of our capital ... and our lovely Arab Gulf. Omar, will you please accompany Mr Makeit?

The following day Dave left – more or less in disgrace. Strangely enough on the same day James was invited by His Excellency to a very luxurious golf club. He stayed a day longer and got a signature on a contract from Mr Ibn Ben Saadi for 6,000 balls with a beep and 2,700 collapsible clubs for the army. James managed to convince Mr Ibn Ben Saadi that the collapsible clubs happened to fit perfectly into the combat packs of the soldiers.

B Task 1: Train your brain

1. What is Mr Ibn Ben Saadi responsible for?

2. Why has Dave joined James in Saudi Arabia?

3. Why is Dave accompanied by Mrs Rubinstein?

4. Why is His Excellency interested in the balls with a beep?

5. Why was the Arab not interested in the golf clubs?

6. How did James manage to sell the clubs after all?

Task 2: Pitfalls for managers

Peter Hayman got an important job with a Saudi oil company. He applied for an employment visa and could bring his wife Jane into the country. Jane had problems adapting to the Arab way of life. She felt isolated and lonely. She could not go to Riyadh on her own to do any shopping nor visit European friends. Women are not allowed to drive a car in Saudi Arabia. After several nervous breakdowns, she booked a flight to London to stay with her parents for a while. At the airport the officials did not allow her to leave the country. Can you imagine why?

FOCUS ON SAUDI ARABIA

 Task 3: Mind your manners

Read the following and find out at least four of Dave's basic mistakes.

Do's
Learn a few polite noises in Arabic.
Accept all invitations.
Take only the food that is offered to you.
Eat with your right hand.
Give your gift in front of others so that there will be no appearance of bribery.
Avoid unpleasant subjects like accidents, poverty, death.
Leave soon after eating.
Praise the country, its food and fashion.

Don'ts
Don't refer to the Gulf as the Persian Gulf. It is the Arab Gulf.
Don't call them Mohammedans, they are Moslems.
Don't shake hands with women.
Don't bring your secretary. It's not a woman's country.
Don't inquire about your host's wives or daughters.
Don't discuss women, politics or religion.
Don't ask them to unpack a present in your presence.
Don't admire your host's pictures, furniture or horses. He might feel obliged to give them to you as a present.
Don't point the sole of your foot towards someone when seated.
Don't touch alcohol; it's against the law.
Don't eat, drink or smoke in public during Ramadan.

 Time for a smile

Who says British companies are inefficient? A British company once took an order to supply 1,800 tons of sand to Abu Dhabi.

Chapter 12

B) Task 4 : Watch their ways

What is typical (T) and what is absolutely untypical (U) of the multi-tasking Arab manager? The first has been done for you.

1. He arrives for the meeting on time. | U |
2. He speaks in a loud voice.
3. He expects you to ask if his family is well.
4. Home is private. He does not invite foreigners to his house.
5. He will stand close to you, touch you and keep eye contact.
6. He will keep his sunglasses on when talking to you.
7. He talks a lot and in a loud voice. It is a sign of strength.
8. Qualified secretaries guarantee that your meeting will not be disturbed by phone calls or visitors.
9. If he accepts you as a friend you can no longer refuse his requests, nor can he yours.

L) Meeting and negotiating with the Arabs

1. Arabs are tough and cautious when it comes to business.
2. Islamic law is the basis of all commercial and social law.
3. They respect the rules of hospitality and religion.
4. Work with an Arab agent who arranges meetings and introduces you to the right persons.
5. Don't conduct business via mail, telephone or fax.
6. Meetings have no fixed beginnings or endings.
7. Begin the meeting with social conversation.
8. Don't rush things, don't press them for an immediate answer.
9. Don't try to finalise a deal at the first meeting.
10. Be patient. Arabs do not keep to the subject.
11. Be prepared for many interruptions.
12. If possible choose the seat next to the most senior person.
13. Try to win his confidence. Do a lot of talking.
14. Discuss the contract as a matter between friends.
15. Keep your word at all times. Personal integrity is as important as facts, figures and profit.

FOCUS ON SAUDI ARABIA 12

(L) Going international: Doing business with Arabs

A market with great potential. The 21 states of the Arab League are an interesting market for European companies. These states cover a territory three times that of Europe and many are rich in oil. Their total population is over 200 million. No Arab constitution is older than 90 years. European managers do not think highly of Arab countries: "Where would they be without their oil?" The Arabs, however have not forgotten that they were once the leading civilisation in the western world. They try to strike a balance between modern technology and their traditions.

Religion influences business. You had better read the Koran if you want to do business with them. In the Gulf States, a good manager is a good Moslem. He will often refer to Allah and the Koran. Islam influences every aspect in the Arab world especially in Saudi Arabia. The Third Development Plan for the Kingdom of Saudi Arabia, 1980-1985 clearly stated: "The distinguishing mark of the Saudi approach to development is that its material and social objectives are derived from the ethical principles of Islam and the cultural values of Saudi society." So your partners and you will often have different views of what is right or wrong. Just because Islam is a fatalistic religion, you should not conclude that Arabs will not buy insurance. Saudi Arabia is a highly competitive insurance market. Over 50 percent of Arab executives have insurance, the rest are so rich, they don't need any.

Communication. They are multi-taskers. They talk about other things before they talk about business. Then after having talked about business they might come back to social matters and so on. The Arab language is a poetic high-context language, rich in associations and allusions. It is important for the native speaker to know how they say what they mean. They tend to overexpress using exaggerations, fantastic metaphors, strings of adjectives and repetitions accompanied by vivid body language. To the Arab, loudness is a sign of strength and sincerity, soft tones imply weakness and lack of sincerity. Remember, the Gulf War took place partly because George Bush spoke softly and Saddam Hussein did not believe what he said about declaring war.

Sources: L. Copeland & L. Griggs and R. L. Lewis

12 Chapter

B Task 5: The travelling manager's country quiz

1. On which day of the week are the shops closed because it is a holy day?
   - a Sunday
   - b Saturday
   - c Friday

2. You can easily hurt your business partner's feelings if you use our Western terminology to refer to his or her country. What should you say instead of
   - a North Vietnam?
   - b Mainland China or Red China (when in China)?
   - c Persian Gulf (when in Saudi Arabia)?
   - d Taiwan (when in China)?

3. What do the Arabs consider offensive?
   - a pointing with your finger
   - b eating with your fingers
   - c pointing the sole of the foot towards someone when seated
   - d talking a lot in a loud voice

4. How do you eat in Saudi Arabia?
   - a Using your right hand.
   - b Keeping your right hand clean; you might have to shake hands with latecomers.
   - c With fork, knife and spoon.

5. Saudis are not Christians. What should you call them?
   - a Mohammedans
   - b Moslems
   - c Islamis

6. How many Arab states are there?
   - a 11
   - b 21
   - c 31

7. How many people live in these states?
   - a 150 million
   - b 200 million
   - c 250 million

8. What is the capital of Saudi Arabia?

FOCUS ON SAUDI ARABIA 12

(V) Vocabulary to help you with the text

accompany	begleiten
administrator	Verwalter
allusion	Anspielung
apologise	sich entschuldigen
attend to someone's needs	sich um jemandes Bedürfnisse kümmern
behaviour	Verhalten, Benehmen
cautious	vorsichtig
combat pack	Sturmgepäck
concept	Vorstellung, Auffassung, Idee
conclude	schließen, folgern
confidence	Vertrauen, Zutrauen
constitution	Verfassung
convince	überzeugen
cover	umfassen, bedecken
declare war on someone	jemandem den Krieg erklären
delicate legs	zarte Beine
depend on eye contact	sich auf Blickkontakt verlassen
desert	Wüste
disgrace; in ~	in Ungnade
distance	Abstand, Entfernung
distinguishing mark	herausragendes Merkmal
disturb	stören
employment visa	Arbeitsvisum
exaggeration	Übertreibung
exit visa	Ausreisevisum
finalize contracts	Verträge abschlußreif machen
fuzz	Flausen, Firlefanz
get hot about	sich über etwas aufregen
hit the bullseye	einen Treffer landen
imminent; an ~ meeting	ein bevorstehendes Treffen
improper dress	unschickliche Kleidung
incomprehensible	unverständlich
insurance	Versicherung
land a contract	einen Vertrag an Land ziehen

Chapter 12

nervous breakdown	Nervenzusammenbruch
objective (n.)	Ziel
offensive (adj.)	beleidigend
pastime	Freizeitbeschäftigung
permission	Erlaubnis
Ramadan	Fastenzeit
recreation facilities	Erholungseinrichtungen
refer to	verweisen, sich beziehen auf
required; be ~ to know	wissen müssen
revenue	Einkommen
sales argument	Verkaufsargument
smooth	glatt, sanft
sole	Sohle
stable	Stall
standards; by American ~	für amerikanische Verhältnisse
starvation	hier: Hungerkuren
strike a balance	Mittelweg finden
support	unterstützen
surprise someone	jemanden überraschen
take for granted	für selbstverständlich halten
take responsibility	Verantwortung übernehmen
talk feelings	Gefühle ansprechen
tough	zäh
trader	Händler
unfamiliar meals	ungewohnte Mahlzeiten
vivid	lebhaft

Chapter 13

FOCUS ON JAPAN
Will we ever understand the Japanese?

🙂 Time for a smile

There was an international computer congress in the USA and the delegates were eating the welcome lunch of the congress.
A Japanese gentleman was sitting next to a delegate from Texas. After the Japanese had finished his soup, the Texan asked him "Likee soupee?" The Japanese nodded. Throughout the meal the American asked such questions as: "Likee fishee?" or "Likee drinkee?"
When the meal was finished the chairman introduced the Japanese gentleman as the guest speaker of the meeting.
The Japanese gentleman rose[1] and gave a witty[2] speech in perfect English. After his speech he returned to his seat and asked the Texan "Likee speechee?"

---

1 rise, rose, risen: aufstehen 2 geistreich

Chapter 13

Will we ever understand the Japanese?

James has just left the airport. He is on his way to the headquarters of Nipon Golf Services which is located in downtown Tokyo.

> James (J), taxi driver (D), girl at the reception (R)

J: Hi, I'd like you to take me to Nipon Golf Services. I have a card here with the street name.

D: Sorry, I cannot read that. It is written in English. Please turn the card over. Ah, here is the Japanese: Nipon Golf Services, Kenichi Yamasaki ... Ah, I know. Please get into the car.

J: Well, thanks. You've been doing this job long?

D: Not too long. I have been with the company twenty-five years.

J: Wow, that's certainly long enough for me. I guess I'll change my company after three or four years.

D: You don't like your work?

J: I sure do. But I've got plans for my career. I've got to climb that ladder. I doubt that sports equipment will satisfy me for long.

D: We've arrived. Here we are. Thank-you.

(Jamie passes through large glass doors to the receptionist.)

R: Can I help you, sir?

J: I sure hope so, miss. I have an appointment with Mr Kenichi.

R: Excuse me, please. I'm new here. The receptionist will be back in a minute. I'm covering for her. If I may have your card, I'll inform Mr Yamasaki that you have arrived.

J: Here you are.

R: Thank-you, Mr ... hmm ... SASL. Would you take a seat, please? Can I arrange for some green tea for you, perhaps?

J: Green tea. Well, I could wash down some good, black coffee, but green tea's not my thing really.

R: Certainly, sir. We have coffee for our international guests.

😊 Japanese wisdom

Traditional: Desire leads to only more desires.
Modernized: Whoever owns a CD-player must buy compact disks.

FOCUS ON JAPAN 13

B Task 1: Train your brain

1. Why did the driver ask James if he didn't like his job?

2. How do Japanese business cards differ from European ones?

3. Have you any idea why the new girl addressed James as Mr SASL?

If you don't know the answers read page 166 before you look at the key.

B Task 2: The one-minute Japanese language trainer

The Japanese have stolen the 'alphabet' from China, car designs from Germany, computers from America, table manners from Britain. Nowadays they are stealing the English language. This helps us to learn Japanese with relative ease. You don't believe it? Here's the proof. You'll have no difficulty matching the English and the Japanese words if you remember the two basic rules:

1. Consonants are separated by vowels.
2. 'R' is pronounced 'L' and 'L' often like 'R'.

And here's your test: Match the English to the Japanese.

1.	beer	a	sarali
2.	radio	b	ah-no-lo-moo-su
3.	salary	c	beelu
4.	enormous	d	hosu-tesu
5.	hostess	e	ladio

☺ Time for a smile

British manufacturers can't win. They produce a new machine and within three months the Russians have invented it, and a month later the Japanese are making it for half the price.

Chapter 13

B) Teaching Japanese how to 'yodel'

You remember the two lingusitic rules?

1. Consonants are separated by vowels.
2. 'R' is pronounced 'L'.

Now let's teach them the Bavarian mountain cry, the 'Yodler'.

1. First, teach them the sentence:

    Do you hold the radio or do I hold the radio

2. Second, make them sing it to the tune of

    Ich hab' mein Herz in Heidelberg verloren ...

3. ... and the Japanese businessmen will yodel:

    Do-you-holudu-ladio-olu-holud-I-ladio
    (repeated seven times.)

B) Task 3: Pitfalls for marketing managers

1. Ford has had a lot of trouble in international markets. It took them some time to find out the reason for the disappointing sales of the Ford Cortina in Japan. Can you imagine why?

2. Pan American Airlines once displayed billboards showing a reclining Japanese woman wearing a kimono. There were complaints. Why?

3. Which colour for high-tech equipment would be a good colour in Japan and a bad colour in the USA?

4. Why is it unwise to name a new car model Silver Ray 4?

5. A company wanted to market intelligent software in Japan. The marketing manager was not sure whether to put the picture of a fox, an owl or an eagle on the package. Which choice would definitely be a bad one?

☺ Japanese proverb

If he works for you, you work for him.

L) Watch their ways: Twelve commandments of Japanese business etiquette

1. The basis of Japanese business etiquette is mutual trust and respect for individuals, companies and values.
2. They are highly status-conscious. Top level executives expect to do business with top level managers from the other company. It is a sign of respect. Never use first names.
3. Before a business relationship can be formed, one must get to know and trust a person.
4. Before you make an appointment send detailed printed information about your company. Your Japanese partners expect you to ask for the same.
5. They do not like newcomers. Make appointments before you arrive in the country. The best way is to be introduced personally by a Japanese agent, or better, by a Japanese business partner.
6. When you are introduced, give them your business card. Cards are also exchanged at parties. You might need up to 30 cards a day. Your cards should be in English and Japanese. You need a qualified professional translator to get it done properly.
7. When offered a business card, do not put it in your pocket. Read it immediately and leave it in front of you on the table.
8. Japanese do not shake hands. If they offer handshakes to westerners it should be followed by a slight bow of your head. Imitate your host. The grip should be gentle.
9. When talking to the Japanese, keep a greater distance than at home. And do not point with your finger, it is impolite. Do not look them straight in the eyes. It is rude.
11. They enjoy offering carefully chosen personal gifts. Westerners are often surprised at the trouble they take to find out about a visitor's family. Follow their example when they visit you.
11. Do not send smart Susan to get the contract. The Japanese Samurai feels uncomfortable in the presence of clever business women who try to negotiate in an aggressive way. Women are rarely invited into the men's social circles.
12. Dress conservatively: Blue or grey suit, white shirt, dark tie. They like clean, not too young, not too hairy, modest and calm business partners.

Chapter 13

Company culture: Understanding the Japanese and ourselves

The western manager	The Japanese manager
1. The company and the individual	
Dave is an individual; that is why he introduces himself as follows: "My name is Dave Makeit, CEO of SASL. Ltd." The company comes last.	Kenichi Yamasaki represents the company. He introduces himself as "Sonya Sports, Marketing Manager, Kenichi Yamasaki." The company comes first.
2. The executive ...	
SASL is run by a boss. He tries to be a charismatic and dominating leader and decision-maker.	Kenichi's firm is run by management groups. The boss hides his ambitions, authority and competence.
3. ... and his employee	
He gives his employee a personal job description and tells him explicitly what to do. He wants his instructions to be executed and he expects results.	He gives vague hints on what to do. Direct orders are offensive. He expects initiative. Job descriptions are for a team, not for an individual.
4. Competitor watch versus customer watch	
He watches his competitor. His strategy is to beat competition by creating a competitive advantage. Competition is a battle. He tries to beat the competitor in any field: prices, development, distribution, design etc.	He watches the customer. He avoids competition by analysing the needs of his customer. The smartest strategy in war is the one that allows you to reach your aim without having to fight.

Source: L. Brennan & D. Block *The Complete Book of Business Etiquette*

A Japanese joke we use over and over

The Italians make the best lovers.
But the Japanese make them smaller and cheaper.

FOCUS ON JAPAN

B Task 4: The travelling manager's country quiz

1. The success of a partnership with a well-established Japanese company is directly related to
   a the image and reputation of their European partner.
   b the conditions you can offer them.
   c the strength of inter-personal relationships.

2. What kind of partnership do Japanese companies prefer to have with foreign companies?
   a They do business on the basis of long-term partnerships.
   b They prefer short-term partnerships to be flexible to changing market situations.

3. Which is the best way to prepare the first meeting?
   a by letter and through personal phone calls.
   b You hire a local agent to arrange an appointment.
   c You go to Japan and arrange it personally. Be patient and have enough time.

4. Don't forget to bring a lot of business cards. How many might you need if you plan to visit two bigger companies?
   a 30   **b** 70   **c** 150

5. What should your business card look like? Will you have it translated into
   a German and English?
   b English and Japanese?
   c German, English and Japanese?

6. Let us compare Japanese and American incomes: How much did Lee Iacocca earn a year at Chrysler?
   a 3 million dollars   **b** 20 million dollars   **c** 30 million dollars

7. Lee Iacocca's income was about one thousand times greater than that of his lowest paid worker. How much more than the lowest paid worker would a Japanese top-manager at a comparable company earn?
   a ten times more   **b** fifty times more   **c** two hundred times more

8. If you want to get on top of business in Japan you had better change your
   a logo   **b** products and services   **c** logo, products, and services

Chapter 13

Vocabulary to help you with the text

advantage	Vorteil
ambition	Ehrgeiz
bow	sich verbeugen
choose, chose, chosen	(aus)wählen
complaint	Beschwerde, Reklamation
desire (n.;v.)	Verlangen, Wunsch; begehren
distance	Abstand, Entfernung
distribution	Verteilung
ease	Leichtigkeit
execute instructions	Anweisungen ausführen
grip	Griff
hairy	haarig
job description	Arbeitsplatzbeschreibung
mutual trust	gegenseitiges Vertrauen
nod	nicken
offensive	beleidigend
owl	Eule
recline	zurückbeugen, -lehnen
rude	unhöflich
status-conscious	statusbewußt
vowel	Vokal

Chapter 14

FOCUS ON JAPAN
Sports articles for the undersized

☺ Time for a smile

An old Japanese general and a diplomat were talking.
"Why do you always win battles[1] whereas[2] we always seem to lose our wars, except[3] the economic ones?" asked the Japanese general.
"Because we always pray[4] to God before we go into a battle," replied the diplomat.
"That's not so, because we also pray to God – but we never win."
"Ah!" said the diplomat, "but not everyone can understand Japanese."

---

1 Schlacht 2 während, wohingegen 3 außer 4 beten

Chapter 14

Sports articles for the undersized

> James (**J**) is led into a large conference room. There he meets Mr Kenichi Yamasaki (**Y**), head of purchasing, two more colleagues in his team, Mr Tohono (**T**) and Mr Dikasaki (**D**).

Y: How do you do? My name is Yamasaki. I'm honored to meet you. May I give you my business card?

J: Sure. *(Puts it in his pocket)* Here's mine. James, James Kelly.

Y: *(Mr Yamasaki takes the card, turns it over and frowns)* And these are colleagues in my group, Mr Tohono and Mr Dikasaki. We're responsible for purchasing in our enterprise.
(James pumps their hands powerfully)

Y: Well, Mr Kelly, I must say we're happy to see you here. We have read your product documentation thoroughly. We were impressed.

J: Great. I can go into some detail about our products.

Y: I believe my colleagues and I would be honored to hear something about yourself and your company.

J: Oh, well sure. SASL, as we call ourselves in short, Sports Aids for Slow Learners was founded eight years ago.

Y: And yourself? How long have you been involved?

J: More than two years. It's a long stint.

Y: Ah, you intend to leave your company at some time in the future?

J: Sure do! Back in the States you need to change companies after three or four years. It's the way to build your career.

Y: Ah, I see. Well, to business. Where would you like to start? Mr Dikasaki, what did we find particularly interesting?

D: We thought the training and equipment package for special learners could be interesting. Who are the special learners?

J: Why, that's you, gentlemen. It's a special package with the following features. You get a bag of clubs which are two thirds the normal length. And they're lighter.

D: What is the reason for that?

J: Your customers are all Japanese. The average height is five feet two inches. The average in Europe or the States is five feet eight inches. So we reduced the length by a third specially for the Japanese market.

Y: Ah, we understand.

J: Then there's the ball. It has a special transmitter inside. You never lose it!

FOCUS ON JAPAN 14

T: And this is specially designed for Japan?
J: Yes, it's two-thirds the normal weight.
T: Because Japanese people are two-thirds as strong as others?
J: Gee, no. It's because you must have a smaller ball if you have a shorter club. It's logical.
T: Ah, I should have realised. Have you other novelties?
J: Just take a look at this ...
J: *(One hour later)* And here's the contract. Black and white. Let's check the details.
Y: Mr Kelly, please do not misunderstand me but here in Japan we prefer to make our arrangements without paper, orally. A person's word is law.
J: Oh, right. Okay well. Hmm, the ball's in your court.
D: You speak of tennis. This does not belong to our theme of today, but we would like to know a little about the offer of your company regarding tennis. Mr Kelly, your company has potential. Think of building a loyal and long-term relationship to it.
J: Sure, I see what you mean ...
D: Would it be a good idea if we had a cup of green tea and considered these things. If you don't object, I'll arrange it.

B Task 1: Train your brain

1. How old is SASL?
2. How long has James been working for Dave?
3. How have clubs and balls been adapted to the Japanese market?

B Task 2: Watch their ways

1. How should James have handled Mr Yamasaki's card?
2. Mr Yamasaki looks at James' card and frowns. Why?
3. What other mistake did James make when introduced to Mr Johono and Mr Dikasaki?
4. There are two facts James should not have mentioned. What are they?

Chapter 14

(L) Meetings the American and the Japanese way

How James Kelly sees it	How Kenichi Yamasaki sees it
1. What they want to get	
James is interested in the current deal that brings instant profit. He would sell his grandmother if the price was right.	Kenichi seeks business relations, profit and market-share in the long-term. He is interested in price, USP and good value for his customers.
2. How they handle time	
He is punctual and works according to schedules and agendas. He expects fast answers and decisions. Long silences are awkward.	He is punctual too. A meeting will go on until the most senior executives interrupts it or a result has been reached. He is a good listener. Long silences show respect.
3. How they open the meeting	
He uses informal small talk and jokes to break the ice, to overcome deadlocks, to put partners at ease or win their confidence.	He gives the impression of being nervous and tense. He wants to find out your motives and whether you are interested in long-term relationships.
4. How they negotiate	
James is an individual. He can negotiate alone, face to face. He can take decisions immediately.	He represents a team. Its members may change from meeting to meeting. He doesn't speak in the first person, he says 'we'.
5. Tactics: Wrestling versus Judo	
James is like a wrestler or a boxer. He trains to build up his intellectual muscles and thinks he can handle small Japanese managers. He tries to defeat by argument.	Kenichi is a Judoka. He uses James' own power to overwhelm him. He gets in line with the direction of James' effort, and simply takes advantage of it.

FOCUS ON JAPAN 14

6. How they handle conflicts

He wants to know where he stands. He is used to dealing with conflicts. Giving in or giving up are signs of weakness. He tries to convince by argument.

He avoids confrontation if it threatens to disturb peace and harmony. Outbreaks of temper and uncontrolled emotions are regarded as a sign of weakness.

7. How they take decisions

Decisions are prepared in meetings. If a result is not achieved the meeting was a failure. Top executives can take lonely decisions and are responsible for them.

Kenichi represents his company's position, therefore, he is less flexible. Decisions are often made by consensus across many management levels at the third or fourth meeting. But then, fast action is expected.

8. How they respect contracts

James prefers written agreements to oral agreements. A deal is a deal when the contract has been signed. Contracts are binding. Do not try to change conditions after you have signed it. Bring your lawyers.

Kenichi prefers oral agreements to written ones. If market or other conditions change he thinks it natural to renegotiate the contract. He doesn't bring his lawyers to the negotiating table. It would be a sign of distrust.

(L) Letter from Japan

Hi Jane,
Well, I got some sort of shock when I arrived here in little old Japan. You look for road signs and directions and you don't even recognize that things are road signs. If you don't speak Japanese you're lost. Fortunately the company I'm checking out lent me one of their employees. He's acting as a sort of guide. I almost can't get rid of him.
They were polite enough in the company. Very polite. I guess they

> were expecting an older man who'd stay with his company all of his life.
> There's another weird thing. In Europe everybody seemed to be offering me baked fish, fried fish, poached fish, grilled fish. In Japan it's all fish, fish, fish, too, but they do it raw. Ugh! Regarding the business I can't tell whether we made an impression or not. At one point I was explaining about the collapsible club when I noticed that the boss seemed to be asleep. I coughed a few times to wake him. It didn't have any effect so I just went on with my presentation. Probably it was all a waste of time. I couldn't get them to sign a contract.
> Tomorrow I'm making a short hop to China. What a market that could be!
>
> Love, Jamie

B Task 3 : More pitfalls for marketing managers

1. Although the Japanese are notoriously camera-loving, they will not buy just any photo-related product. One US company was about to sell desk-top photograph displays to managers. They soon found out that in Japan this would be a flop. Why?

2. An American executive in Japan wanted to motivate his sales force by introducing the American bonus system. The company's most successful salesman and his family would be sent on a holiday abroad. The Japanese salesmen were not interested. Why?

3. An American manager was making a presentation to a team of Japanese executives. His audience was listening in silence, did not take notes, did not interrupt nor did they ask questions. He was getting more and more nervous. When he realised that some of them seemed to have fallen asleep he knew that the deal was lost. What is your comment?

FOCUS ON JAPAN 14

B Task 4: The travelling manager's country quiz

1. Why do Japanese and Korean car manufacturers produce different models for different countries to fit the tastes of overseas customers, whereas BMW and Mercedes don't?

    a BMW and Mercedes are not as flexible as Japanese manufacturers.

    b BMW and Mercedes are in a well-defined, up-market segment.

    c The Asian manufacturers cater to the lower and middle classes.

2. Japanese companies have the reputation of being innovative. NEC, for example, launches a new product every two or three months. Tick off those strategies that you think might explain this.

    a They concentrate on one single project at a time.

    b They pursue dozens of different projects at a time.

    c They invest more money in R&D.

    d They avoid unnecessary red tape.

    e Their engineers are better trained.

3. Japanese marketing techniques have found a lot of imitators. They have not only adopted the strategies, but also the vocabulary. Match the Japanese expressions and their English equivalents:

    1 kaizen   **a** financial engineering

    2 jit   **b** quality control

    3 zaitech   **c** just in time management

4. Why does Volkswagen sell Nissan four-wheel-drive cars? Why does Nissan do the same for VW in Japan?

    a They own equity in each other's companies. It's a joint venture.

    b They do not want to invest in distribution systems.

    c They share the profits.

Chapter 14

5. The American Government urged the Japanese government to import more beef from the United States. The Japanese Government had several strategies to choose from. Which do you think they have decided to adopt?

   a They rear the cattle in Japan but agree to import the feed from the United States.
   b They import the beef if the price is right.
   c They buy farms in the USA and buy the beef from their own companies.

6. In the USA it is advisable to bring lawyers to the negotiating table. What about Japan?

   a Bring your lawyers. Japanese business persons do it, too.
   b Bring your lawyers. They want to finalise contracts down to the last detail.
   c Don't. Japanese business partners might be offended.

7. What do the Japanese mean when they say 'hai' (yes)?

   a How interesting. I'm all ears.
   b I agree. It's a deal.
   c I'm afraid, I can't follow you.

8. You should know a few words of Japanese. Match the English and Japanese expressions:

1 Good day		a komban wa'
2 Good bye		b 'onegai'
3 Good evening		c kon-nichi wa'
4 Please		d sayonara

9. How many people do these Japanese companies employ in the UK?

   a 100,000   b 200,000   c 300,000

FOCUS ON JAPAN 14

(V) Vocabulary to help you with the text

achieve a result	ein Ergebnis erzielen
adopt a strategy	Strategie übernehmen
average height	durchschnittliche Größe
avoid	vermeiden
beef	Rindfleisch
bonus system	Prämiensystem
cater to	beliefern, bedienen
comparable	vergleichbar
confidence	Vertrauen
consider things	die Dinge überdenken
convince	überzeugen
current deal	das laufende Geschäft
deadlock	toter Punkt, Pattsituation
defeat	besiegen
directly related to	direkt bezogen auf
disturb peace	den Frieden stören
ear; I'm all ears	ich bin ganz Ohr
enterprise	Unternehmen, Firma
feature	Eigenschaft, Merkmal
finalise a contract	einen Vertrag zum Abschluß bringen
frown	die Stirn runzeln
head of purchasing	Einkaufsleiter
honored; I'm ~ to meet you	es ist mir eine Ehre, Sie kennenzulernen
in the long term	langfristig, auf lange Sicht
income	Einkommen
intend	beabsichtigen
involved; how long have you been ~ ?	wie lange sind Sie schon dabei?
it's a long stint	es ist eine lange Zeit
lighter	leichter
manufacturing plant	Produktionsstätte, Fabrik
negotiate	verhandeln
novelty	Neuheit
offend	beleidigen

Chapter 14

oral agreement	mündliche Vereinbarung
outbreaks of temper	Gefühlsausbrüche
photograph display	Fotorahmen (für Schreibtische)
punctual	pünktlich
red tape	Bürokratie, Papierkram
reduce the length by ...	um ... verkürzen
renegotiate	neu verhandeln
silence	Stille, Schweigen
take advantage of	ausnutzen
tense	angespannt, nervös
thoroughly	gründlich
threaten	drohen
transmitter	Sender
undersized	zu klein
up-market segment	Marktsegment am oberen Ende der Preisskala
USP (unique selling point)	einzigartiges Verkaufsargument
weight	Gewicht
wrestler	Ringer

☺ Time for a smile

Golf is a good walk spoiled.
Mark Twain

Chapter 15

FOCUS ON CHINA
The Chinese Connection

🙂 Time for a smile

There is an ancient Chinese ceremony in which the parents of a child choose the baby's name:
As soon as the baby is born, all the cutlery[1] in the house of its parents is thrown in the air. The parents then listen to the falling knives, forks, and spoons and choose a name: ping, peng, boing, cheung ...

---

1 Besteck

Chapter 15

The China connection

Business is going to be a little different in the People's Republic of China since James has to deal with the state itself and not with a private company. He had some difficulties in finding the right partners. After five days, he is invited to a small but well lit, local restaurant. It smells of a thousand different Chinese curries and peppers.

> He is welcomed by Mr Lee (L) who is director of pastimes and entertainments for the Canton. In the room several people are standing around including Mr Tai-li (T), the regional party secretary.

L: On behalf of my team I would sincerely like to welcome you to Beijing. May I present myself, my name is Lee, Mr Wang, my assistant and our honoured guest from the Ministry, Mr Tai-li? *(They all bow to James, who bows back.)*

J: Gentlemen, the honour is all mine. Here's my business card and please allow me to offer you all a small gift from my company. *(James hands each of them a bottle of the best old bourbon whisky. The three gentlemen are somewhat confused and even embarrassed.)*

L: Mr Kelly, that was not at all necessary. It is not our custom.

J: Just forget all about it, Gentlemen, let's just say it's the American way. Well, I'm so happy to be here. I've been looking forward to seeing your country. I can tell you I have spent a lot of time checking up on Mainland China. I've really got into Chinese culture and especially the food side of it.

T: Of course, we ourselves would prefer to initiate you in the ways of Chinese culture and certainly of our cuisine. Firstly, on behalf of those here I would like to make a toast to you. *(In front of Jamie on the table is a small pot with rice wine in it.)* May you and your family prosper and may you enjoy good health.

J: Well, thank-you kindly, Gentlemen and the same to yourselves. *(Everybody suddenly starts clapping.)* Wow! What did I do? It wasn't that great.

L: Sir, please accept another pot of rice wine from our humble selves. May I?

J: My God, no! I wouldn't be able to think straight after another glass and then I wouldn't be able to get my prices right anymore.

L: *(Obviously a little surprised)* Please accept my apologies. It is our custom to please our guests.

J: No problem, folks. Well, perhaps we ought to be getting ...

T: If you would permit a small suggestion from our side. We had thought that a small test of our culture in the form of good and typical cuisine might relax us all before we begin the discussions on the sports equipment. You said you had learned a lot about our food. What are your favourite things?

J: Well, Gentlemen, certainly not snakes or monkeys' brains. And I'm not very keen on fish nowadays, either.

L: *(A little surprised)* These thing are considered by some to be a delicacy.

J: No, sirs, I can't eat that at all. What about a good sharp curried beef?

B Task 1: Train your brain cross-culturally

First read the Ten Commandments of Chinese business etiquette on the next page. Then find the five commandments James has violated.

B Task 2: President Reagan's mistake

President Reagan made headlines on his 1984 trip to China when he overpaid a souvenir. "Keep the change," he said as he walked away. Humiliated the shopkeeper ran after him to return the money. What went wrong?

Source: Copeland & Griggs

☺ Food for thought

When a diplomat says yes, he means maybe;
if he says maybe, he means no;
if he says no, he is no diplomat.

Chapter 15

 Watch their ways: Ten commandments of Chinese business etiquette

1. Offer gifts in private, not in front of others, as in Arab countries.
2. Don't imitate your Chinese partners. Be yourself!
3. Don't show off your knowledge about Chinese culture and traditions even if you think you are an expert on Chinese affairs. (By the way, you are not and will never be one). They might interpret it as western arrogance. Be modest! Make excuses that you don't know much about their culture. They will forgive you.
4. In China a wise man knows how to shut up. Don't talk too much!
5. As a visitor you offer your business card first. Do it with both hands. If offered a business card, hold it with both hands and pretend to read it carefully even if you don't understand a word.
6. When an Asian smiles it could be a signal that he is embarrassed about some bad news.
7. If a toast is made, there will be a clapping of hands. Clap back and smile.
8. Dress conservatively and more formally than you would at home.
9. Don't refuse food or drinks. Your host will be offended. Learn to eat with chop sticks. Don't be afraid – it's a good omen if you drop them on the floor.
10. Don't refer to China as Mainland China. It is the People's Republic of China. And Taiwan is not a sovereign state but one of the Republic's provinces.

 Mind your manners

What you should not say in China.

- → Not bad for a man of your size.
- → Why can't you speak plopel English?
- → Why can't you write like everybody else?
- → I'm going to see my friends in Taiwan next week.
- → Why can't you give me a simple yes or no?

FOCUS ON CHINA

(L) Going international: Ten golden rules on your way to China

1. Although the Republic is communist, it is not an egalitarian society. Stability is based on inequality and respect of unequal relationships. People don't question the authority of the leader, the son obeys his father, the younger brother respects his elder brother. It is quite natural that managers have privileges.
2. Western companies can save weeks and months of time if they have the right agent in Hong Kong, Taiwan or China.
3. Like in Japan you need a letter of introduction written by the right person to open the right doors. It should be signed by a respected high-ranking person. His status and prestige will be yours.
4. Don't say no. Say "I'll see what I can do…" or "I'll think it over …"
5. Don't rush it. The worst thing to say to a Chinese or a Japanese at a meeting is "Give me a simple yes or no."
6. Everybody's face must be saved.
7. If you want to impress them wear a Rolex rather than a Timex. Some Chinese might know the difference.
8. Do not rely on their interpreter. He is a source of misunderstandings. Bring your own interpreter, a Chinese of the region who is bilingual and knows your company and your products.
9. Learn a few words of Chinese to be able to make polite noises. It's good if you know enough Mandarin to understand what your partners and your interpreter say. Don't try to speak it, even if you are under the illusion that you can. They won't appreciate your accent.
10. Don't expect that there will be a typewriter, fax or telex at the hotel. And if there is, your fax or telex will be read by a party official. By the way, you should offer your partners fax or telex machines to improve further communication. It is worth the investment.

☺ Time for a smile

Chancellor Kohl describing his visit in China:
"We went riding in one of those rickshaws", he told his wife, "and believe it or not, they have horses that look just like men."

Chapter 15

B A cross-cultural checklist

Personal experience is worth ten golden rules. So when you go on a business-trip to an Asian country make notes of cultural differences in business. Here is a checklist for you and your employees.

Differences	How I noticed them	How they affected my job
Appointments		
Business cards		
Correspondence		
Working hours		
Meetings		
Negotiations		
Decision-making		
Hospitality		
Presents		

☺ Time for a smile

During his stay in Peking James heard the following joke:
When Brent Scowcroft, the national security advisor of US President Bush, was visiting China, he brought a special telephone along for Deng Xiaoping. With this telephone it was possible to get into contact with every living and dead person from past, present and future. Deng's first three telephone calls: first with President Bush in Washington to thank him for the wonderful present. Then with his dead comrade in heaven, Chou Enli. And finally with Mao-Tse-Tung in hell.
One month later Deng got his telephone bill. He noticed only two long-distance calls had been invoiced – the one to Washington, the other to heaven. So he phoned the telephone company to find out why he had not been billed for his call to Mao. The voice at the other end answered: "Hell is a local call."

FOCUS ON CHINA 15

Ⓛ Going international: About time, patience and gifts

How they see themselves. Westerners see China as a Third World underdeveloped country. They forget that it is also the oldest civilisation on earth that invented gun powder and porcelain at a time when Europeans were still throwing stones at each other. They civilised Japan and all their neighbouring nations. They see themselves as the middle Empire, the centre of the universe which might become the planet's biggest future market.

How to prepare the trip. You must be invited to trade with China. The bureaucratic machinery is very slow. Presents are risky and tipping is officially discouraged. If you want to make a present do it publicly at banquets so that it cannot be misunderstood as a bribe. Since customs officials are very suspicious you had better bring out of the country everything you take in with you, or you might be suspected of bribery. They do not trust us westerners who, in some parts of China, are still considered as 'foreign devils'.

Take your time and be patient. Be prepared for endless delays in all phases of business because in China time is relative, which the following story shows: A Chinese official informed an ARCO manager that tomorrow China would be the number one nation in the world. The American said that he did not doubt it, considering the size of the country and its population and the tremendous technical progress that will be made, but he asked, "When do you think that China will become number one?" The Chinese answered, "Oh, in four or five hundred years."

So be patient when doing business in China; how patient will be illustrated by this story. A young Chinese was called to his boss who was to retire soon. The old man asked him if he was ready to take his position in the communist party. The young man was overjoyed. "One thing you must remember when dealing with people," said the old man, "always be patient." The young man nodded. The old man repeated his advice three times, when he was going to repeat it a fourth time the young man said "Do you take me for an idiot? Why do you repeat such a simple thing four times?" The old man smiled and said "I've only said it a few times, and you're already impatient."

Chapter 15

B Task 3: The manager's key to the Great Wall of China

1. Your agent has been negotiating a deal with a group of mainland Chinese officials for a couple of weeks. He writes that they will come to your country to finalise the contract. One month later they have still not given you a date for their arrival. What will you do?
   - **a** Forget the deal?
   - **b** Wait?

2. You are getting nervous and impatient. Could it be that they are expecting something from you?
   - **a** the tickets for the plane
   - **b** official invitation in writing
   - **c** a confirmation of the deal from the Chinese embassy

3. Might it be an idea to go to the People's Republic of China as a sign of respect?
   - **a** Do you travel to China?
   - **b** Do you go on waiting?

4. What type of negotiators will sit down at the conference table with you?
   - **a** specially trained negotiators and experts
   - **b** people with a career in the communist party rather than experts
   - **c** people with a degree from a western university

5. Who is the boss? Who decides whether you get the contract?
   - **a** The highest-ranking executive in the company.
   - **b** The oldest and most experienced executive.
   - **c** The one with an uncle in the ministry.

6. Which is a bad month in which to negotiate with Chinese partners?
   - **a** July
   - **b** April, November
   - **c** end of January, first week of February

FOCUS ON CHINA

(V) Vocabulary to help you with the text

advice	Ratschlag
affect	beeinträchtigen, beeinflussen
Beijing	Peking
bill someone	jemandem etwas in Rechnung stellen
bribe	Bestechung
chop sticks	Eßstäbchen
considering	in Anbetracht
custom	Brauch, Sitte
customs official	Zollbeamter
delay (n.; v.)	Verzögerung; verzögern
describe	beschreiben
embarrassed	verlegen
entertaining	Bewirtung
finalise the contract	den Vertrag zum Abschluß bringen
get into something	sich anfreunden mit
gift	Geschenk
humble; our ~ selves	unsere Wenigkeiten
humiliate	erniedrigen, demütigen
impatient	ungeduldig
improve	verbessern
inequality	Ungleichheit
initiate	beginnen, initiieren
invoice (n.; v.)	Rechnung; berechnen
keen; be ~ on	scharf sein auf
look forward to	sich freuen auf
modest	bescheiden
monkeys' brains	Affenhirn
obey	gehorchen
offended; be ~	beleidigt sein
overjoyed	überglücklich
pastime	Freizeitaktivität
prosper	gedeihen
question the authority	die Autorität in Frage stellen
refuse food	Essen ablehnen

Chapter 15

shut up	den Mund halten
size	Größe
snakes	Schlangen
suspicious	argwöhnisch; verdächtig
think straight	klar denken
tipping	Trinkgeld geben
tremendous	riesig
violate a commandment	gegen ein Gebot verstoßen

☺ Time for a smile

China has a great team of female swimmers. Their coach answers to the name[1] of Do Ping.

---

1 hört auf den Namen

FOCUS ON CHINA
Singing balls and propaganda

Chapter 16

☺ How to say 'No' the Chinese way

Here is an example of how frustrating Chinese politeness can be:

A Beijing paper rejected[1] a British journalist's manuscript:
"We have read your manuscript with boundless delight[2]. If we were to publish your paper, it would be impossible to publish any work of a lower standard. And as it is unthinkable that, in the next thousand years, we shall see its equal[3], we are, to our regret, compelled[4] to return your divine[5] composition, and beg you a thousand times to overlook our short sightedness and timidity[6]."

Source: Lennie Copeland, Lewis Griggs, *Going International*

---

1 ablehnen 2 grenzenloses Entzücken 3 seinesgleichen 4 zwingen 5 göttlich
6 Verzagtheit, Schüchternheit

Chapter 16

Singing balls and propaganda

> James has to wait another three days before he is invited to the second meeting in a huge grey building. He is shown into a tiny conference room. Three Chinese officials, Mr Lin Yu Tang (T) and Mr Lin Enlai (L), a gentleman of about 80 years, are sitting round a table obviously waiting for something. Confused, James looks around. No familiar faces. "I'm at the wrong meeting," he thinks. Lin Yu Tang rises to welcome James.

T: Come in, come in Mr Kelly. May I introduce myself? My name is Lin Yu Tang, Mr Lee's secretary. I would like you to meet Mr Liu Shaoqi, the coach of the army's golf team and Mr Lin Enlai who is in charge of the sports facilities for retired party officials.

J: Excuse me gentleman, but I was expecting to meet Mr Lee and his colleagues.

T: We beg you not to trouble yourself about this situation. We are here to learn more about the products Mr Lee has told us so much about.

J: Well, I can certainly fill you in on what we've worked out for you. You remember that we described it in the documentation you received from us. Well, I've a sample here. Now, if you'll just come out into the courtyard. I need some space for the demonstration.
(James takes them outside, swings at the ball which jumps down a drain.)

J: Now, we've lost the ball. You're getting desperate, you're worried about wasting time. What do you do?

T: Take another golf-ball?

J: Not a chance. You press this button on your wrist-band and you immediately get a melody together with some information. Listen!
(James clicks the button and suddenly from the lost golf-ball the sweet melody of Stars and Stripes, the American national anthem, pipes forth.)

T: Mr Kelly! Please switch off that decadent music.

J: Don't worry! That was a small mistake with the electronics. Now your personal singing golf-ball is really special. Customised for you. I pressed the wrong button. Moreover, gentlemen, we can fit any slogan or propaganda you want into the golf-ball. What do you think of that?

(He presses another button, and the anthem of the People's Republic of China is piped forth.)

T: Mr Kelly, I have no words.

J: Don't worry, the golf-ball has words enough. And now I'd like to explain about our special golf-clubs. Please look at this club. Isn't it ...? *(James explains and explains and explains ...).*

J: *(fade in)* ... and so Gentlemen, I really feel that the collapsible golf-club, perhaps even the super short one and our "singing" golf-ball which always leads you back to it, would be a big hit in your country. Concerning prices I'd only like to say that our prices, considering the quality, are about ...

T: We are sure, My Kelly that your prices are fair. However, we would ask you to take into account the matter of number. The People's Republic is without doubt your largest potential market. If we take up business with you, the business may be as much as you do with the rest of the world together.

J: Jesus, that's right. Well, you know what we say. "Think big and you'll be big", or something like that.

L: And then one should think of the courses all over the province.

J: Didn't get that one, Gentlemen. What courses?

L: The golf courses which still need to be designed and planned plus the training of staff so they can teach the hundreds of thousands of potential customers. Mr Kelly, you have gone pale. These things are part of your service, are they not?

J: You can bet your bottom dollar! Say, any more of that rice wine available?

B Task 1: Train your brain

1. Why did the ball play the wrong anthem?
2. Why did Mr Lin Yu Tang say, "Mr Kelly, I have no words"?
3. Why did James go pale and ask for more rice wine?
4. "We would ask you to take into account the matter of number", said Mr Lin Yu Tang. What was his intention?

Chapter 16

Going international: Meetings the Chinese way

A German manager once said that western negotiators in China are thankful to get out with the shirts on their backs. If they do not know when to break off negotiations and take the next plane home, they will lose everything including their minds. Here is some good advice for your meetings:

1. Bring enough time. You might have to wait for days before meeting the right people.
2. Your partners will arrive 15 minutes before the appointed time.
3. Meetings are formal. Show respect for the senior members.
4. Seating will be according to hierarchy.
5. No jokes to break the ice. You don't understand Chinese humour, they don't understand western jokes.
6. They place values and principles above money.
7. You might be a good businessman and negotiator. However, if you are not technically competent and not familiar with details, they will not respect you as a competent businessman.
8. Bring a team of experts.
9. Chinese are group-orientated. Like the Japanese they do not say "I think ... " but "We think ..."
10. In following meetings you might have to deal with different partners.
11. Take your time and negotiate step by step. You will need a lot of patience.
12. They combine flexibility with firmness.
13. They expect to get lower prices than other countries because China is such a big market.
14. The meeting is for gathering information. Decisions will be taken outside the meeting.
15. Decisions are made with a view to the long term, not to the short term.
16. No formal agreement exists without a written contract.
17. They expect reliability and punctual delivery.

Source: Richard D. Lewis, *When Cultures Collide*

FOCUS ON CHINA 16

B Task 2: Watch their ways

Now let us see how good your memory is. How many of the 17 Chinese negotiating habits mentioned in the list on page 192 do you recognize in James' second meeting with the Chinese? The first has been done for you:

Number 1: Bring enough time. You might have to wait for days before meeting the right people.
There are four more for you to find.

B Task 3: Patchwork – Words negotiators will use

customised   to learn more   part of
was expecting   fill you in on
long-term business   take up   potential market
account   not to trouble

Can you put the patches in the right places?

1. Excuse me gentlemen, but I .... to meet Mr Lee and his colleagues.
2. We beg you .... yourself about this situation.
3. We are here .... about the products.
4. I can certainly .... what we've worked out for you.
5. Now your singing golf-ball is specially .... for you.
6. We would hope for .... with your company.
7. We would ask you to take into .... the matter of number.
8. The Peoples' Republic is your largest ....
9. If we .... business with you, it may be as much as you do with the rest of the world.
10. These things are .... your service, are they not?

Chapter 16

(L) Watch their ways – read their minds

Let's read James' mind	Let's read Mr Lee's mind
Time is money.	Time is time and money is money.
I'm going to the meeting to find out Mr Chu's position and aims.	I'm trying to find out James' position and aims before the meeting.
When I say "no", I mean "no".	No means "I'll do my best".
A contract is the beginning of a business relationship.	A contract is the beginning of a personal relationship.
I've got the deal when I've got the signature. The written contract is binding.	Oral agreements are part of the contract and as reliable as a written one.
The truth is the truth.	The truth is the truth if it is sociologically acceptable and the Communist Party agrees.
I'll set him an ultimatum otherwise we'll never get anywhere.	Ultimatum? What a rude fellow! I'd lose face if I accepted it.
He smiles so he seems to have swallowed it.	This ultimatum is very embarrassing indeed. Keep smiling, Chu.
A joint venture means getting a firm foothold in the biggest market on this planet.	We'll get Western capital and know-how. When the production plant is built, we'll run it ourselves.
Mr Lee is a nice guy. I think we'll be good friends one day. I'll invite him over to the States.	James is a nice guy. He'll invite me over to the States. As a friend he will lodge my son and pay the university fees for him.

☺ Time for a smile

The Great Wall, I've been told, is the only man-made structure that is visible from the moon. For the life of me, I cannot see why anyone would go to the moon to look at it, when, with almost the same difficulty, it can be viewed in China.

J.K. Galbraith

FOCUS ON CHINA

L) Letter from behind the Great Wall

Hi there, Jane,

Me Tarzan! Gee, it feels like I've been away a long time. And I'm fed up with all this rice and fish. You know I don't really have anybody to relate to here. I'm having quite a few meetings but the managers change every time. It's like musical chairs only I'm the chair. Oh yeah, I wanted to complain to Dave about the electronics in the singing golf balls. The foolish sphere started singing our American song. The Chinese almost went emotional about it.

Speaking of feelings you know I'm rather looking forward to seeing you again. But it won't be for a while. Dave has been so serious since the fiasco in Saudi Arabia. And now he says we're not really international if we don't go to South America. I mean, who does business in South America? And what about the crime? And the terrorists? They'll have the shirt off my back. So Tuesday next week I'll be in Mexico.

Love, Jamie

P.S. How are you getting along with Dave in your new company? I get the feeling he almost wants me out of the way in South America. Don't forget to fax me the travel notes for Mexico.

B) Task 4: The manager's key to the Great Wall of China

1. The time has come to sign the contract. Is it advisable to bring your lawyers to see that all the conditions are watertight?

   a Yes, because Chinese businessmen prefer vague and general formulations.

   b Yes, because Chinese negotiators want to stipulate even the smallest details.

   c No, because a contract is an agreement between gentlemen. Personal relations are more important than contracts.

16 Chapter

2. What does the typical Chinese modesty really mean?
- **a** It is a weapon in negotiations.
- **b** It is a sign of good character.
- **c** It is a form of politeness.

3. His name is Lin Wu. How do you address him?
- **a** Mr Lin Wu
- **b** Mr Lin
- **c** Mr Wu
- **d** Lin Wu san

4. How do you greet a Chinese business partner?
- **a** You shake hands.
- **a** You bow.

5. A Texan manufacturer asked a Chinese consultant what to offer to a higher-ranking executive from mainland China. What do you think the answer was?
- **a** Cigarettes and a bottle of fine old whisky.
- **b** A Cartier fountain pen and ballpoint.
- **c** A pair of fine leather cowboy boots produced by one of his companies, with the American and Chinese flags on them.

6. There are strong Chinese communities in San Francisco, London, Singapore and of course in Hongkong and Taiwan.
- **a** Do they still feel as one nation with one cultural background?
- **b** Have they lost their links to mainland China?

7. Why do the Chinese prefer to do business with big, well-known companies rather than with smaller companies whose products and prices are better?
- **a** Chinese officials have little experience of the international market. They only know the multi-national companies.
- **b** Big companies are more stable and reliable.
- **c** Big companies have more prestige.

FOCUS ON CHINA 16

8. Your Chinese business partners have finally signed the contract and to celebrate the occasion they invite you to an elegant Beijing wine restaurant. Among the Chinese waitresses there is a young, particularly beautiful girl. Can you invite her to your hotel room for a 'tête à tête'?

> **a** Don't! You are not in a Bangkok brothel! You might spend a few nights in a Chinese prison cell and be put on the next plane home.
>
> **b** Well, if there is no lady among your business partners, they might see no harm in having *'hao shi'* (love and sex) with the waitress.

9. During the meal you drop your chop sticks. They fall on the floor.

> **a** This is a catastrophe. The Chinese are superstitious and see it as a bad omen for a business partnership.
>
> **b** It is a good omen: you will be invited a second time.

(V) Vocabulary to help you with the text

aim	Ziel
break off negotiations	Verhandlungen abbrechen
brothel	Bordell
button	Knopf
chop sticks	Eßstäbchen
concerning prices	was die Preise betrifft
courtyard	Hof
customised	maßgeschneidert
desperate	verzweifelt
drain	Abfluß
familiar; be ~ with	vertraut sein mit
fed; be ~ up with	die Nase voll haben von
fill someone in on	jemanden informieren
firmness	Festigkeit
gather information	Informationen sammeln
lodge	unterbringen

modesty	Bescheidenheit
musical chairs	die Reise nach Jerusalem
national anthem	Nationalhymne
obviously	offensichtlich
pale; go ~	blaß werden
pipe forth music	Musik erklingen lassen
place principles above money	Prinzipien über Geld stellen
prefer	vorziehen
pushy	aufdringlich, aggressiv
relate to someone	hier: mit jemandem reden
retired party officials	pensionierte Parteifunktionäre
sample	Muster
senses	Sinne, Verstand
sphere	Kugel
step by step	Schritt für Schritt
stipulate even the smallest details	selbst die kleinsten Details festlegen
swallow the ultimatum	das Ultimatum schlucken
take into account	in Betracht ziehen, berücksichtigen
take up business	Geschäftsbeziehungen aufnehmen
values	Werte
waitress	Kellnerin
watertight conditions	hieb- und stichfeste Bedingungen
weapon	Waffe
with a view to	mit Aussicht auf
without doubt	zweifelsohne
wrist-band	Armband

Chapter 17

FOCUS ON SOUTH AMERICA
Love's labour lost in Mexico?

🙂 Time for a smile

The bar of the Hotel Montezuma was crowded. As there was only one empty chair at the table of an elderly Mexican businessman James bowed and said, "Kelly, James Kelly." The gentleman rose, bowed and said, "Buenos Dias".
The next morning James met the Mexican at breakfast. He bowed and said, "Buenos Dias". James smiled and replied, "Kelly, James Kelly." When James met the friendly gentleman at lunchtime, the same ceremony happened again. The waiter who was serving them explained to James, "Buenos Dias is not his name, you understand. He is only saying Good morning." James was grateful and when he met the Mexican again at dinner he said "Buenos dias". The Mexican, pleased to see that James had taken the trouble to learn the language replied, "Kelly, James Kelly."

Chapter 17

 Love's labour lost in Mexico?

> We are in Mexico. A lot of strange things have happened to Jamie. He feels dreadful. He phones up Dave in the States.

J: Hi Dave, it's me. My god, I'm in all sorts of trouble. Can you come down?

D: James, normally you've got to take care of it yourself.

J: I know, I know. Dave, you wouldn't believe what's been going on. I've been with the police the best part of two days. I ...

D: Okay, okay, I've got some points as well.

J: Great! I didn't expect you to ...

D: No problem. See you in your hotel bar at 5 p.m. tomorrow evening.

J: Wow, that's quick. How can you get here so quickly?

D: Oh, I've been having a short vacation with a friend in California.

J: Good for you, Dave. Do I know her?

D: Well, you ... let's talk about it in Mexico City.

(Clinking of glasses in the bar of the Hotel Montezuma)

J: My god, I'm glad you're here, Dave. It's unbelievable!

D: Now, take it easy, James. There's something I'd like to ...

J: Oh, don't worry. Listen to my story. Your hair'll stand on end.

D: Okay, okay, guess my stuff's not so important. Shoot!

J: So, I arrived at the airport, rented a large car to keep all the SASL gear in. Well, I was driving along peacefully when suddenly ...

D: You had a crash?

J: Not exactly. It was the car behind me. You see, a cow walked across the road and I had to hit the brakes.

D: You didn't want to kill the animal?

J: I didn't want to damage the car.

D So what's the problem? Did you kill the animal?

J: No, but I damaged the car. The rear lights were broken.

D: So the fool behind you had to pay.

J: Gee, Dave, it's not so easy.

D: It's very clear as far as I can see! The one who hits you from behind is ...

J: Dave, it was the police. It was a large truck carrying a lot of police horses. Jesus, the cops in the truck were really friendly.

FOCUS ON MEXICO 17

D: No surprise, since they caused the accident.

J: Okay. I went to the police station with them. I was there more than six hours, drinking strong coffee. They were very friendly. I was introduced to more than 20 horses. I reckon they speak better English than the Mexicans.

D: But you got out in the end?

J: Yeah, but what a waste of time.

D: Why?

J: They gave me a document for my damages. Then they told me it wasn't worth a dime. I should go to the office of the Traffic Police to get some more papers.

D: So, did you get the papers?

J: Dave, I drove there. An interpreter explained everything to the traffic cops.

D: So, no problem!

J: Not quite, Dave! First, they wanted to see the offending car, the police truck. Well, of course, that wasn't there. Next I had to give them my car papers.

D: So! That was no problem, was it?

J: Christ, yes it was. They were so friendly. I got one of the best espressos I've ever drunk.

D: Well?

J: Don't you remember our company rule? When travelling deposit your vital documents at the bank! I did just that. But the traffic police wanted originals. So, they confiscated the car.

D: James, you got the car back, didn't you?

J: Sure did, Dave.

D: Well, everything's apple pie then, isn't it?

J: I sure got the car back. That's right.

D: Well, what's your problem?

J: It's our problem, Dave. You remember the SASL equipment in the trunk of the car. It's gone.

D: What do you mean 'gone'?

J: I mean somebody removed it. Somebody stole it.

D: Oh, my god! Those were prototypes, worth thousands.

J: You got it, Dave. Now tell me about that girl, your Californian friend.

Chapter 17

B Task 1: Train your brain

More than one answer may be right.

1. Why was Dave willing to see James in Mexico City?
    - a He wanted to spend a holiday there with his new girl friend.
    - b He was in California anyway.
    - c He wanted to discuss a few points with James.

2. How did the car accident happen?
    - a James did not want to knock a cow over.
    - b A truck crashed into his car.
    - c He tried to avoid some cops on horses.

3. What reasons did the police give for confiscating the car?
    - a They did not accept the photocopies of the car papers.
    - b Dave had deposited all his documents at the bank.
    - c They did it because they don't like Yankees.

For the following two questions, make use of your imagination.

4. How might James have spared himself all the trouble with the police?

5. What are the "few points" Dave did not want to discuss on the phone?

B Task 2: Pitfalls for managers

When a rich vein of gold was found in a Latin-American country, Americans and French wanted to develop the mining. The French had no problem to hire workers among the local population. The Americans, however, had difficulties finding workers, although they offered regular working hours, better housing and better working conditions. Do you know why the Americans failed?

Source: Lennie Copeland, Lewis Griggs, *Going International*
Richard L. Lewis *When Cultures Collide*

FOCUS ON MEXICO

(L) **Going international:**
If you know one Latin country, you know them all

Leadership. In Latin Europe, as well as in South America, the management pattern generally follows that of France, where authority is centred around the chief executive. In middle-sized companies, the CEO is very often the owner of the enterprise and even in very large firms a family name may dominate the structure. More than in France, sons, nephews, cousins and close family friends will hold key positions.

Management. Status is based on age, reputation and often on wealth. The management style is as autocratic as it is in Spain or Portugal where family money is often in the company. There is a growing meritocracy in Brazil, Chile and in the big northern Italian industrial firms. Task orientation is dictated from above, strategies and success depend largely on social and ministerial connections and mutually beneficial cooperation between dominant families. Knowing the right people oils the wheels of commerce in Latin countries.

Negotiating. They are status-conscious. The first contact should never be made by a low-level expert. Women are generally, although not always, excluded from negotiating sessions. Americans tend to skip the preliminary posturing. Mexicans, however, like opening talks with lengthy conversation, but little substance. They are more affective than logic: emotion and drama carry more weight.
Early concessions and compromises are not virtues in Mexico, Russia, Arabia. The Mexican will not compromise as a matter of honour, dignity and integrity. Personal relationships are essential to business. Many of Mexican business negotiations will centre on personal aspects like trust. Different from Japan, you should get the results confirmed in writing since verbal agreement may be reached out of politeness, only to be reversed later by letter.

Source: L. Copeland & L. Griggs and
R. L. Lewis

Chapter 17

Fax From America

Hi James,

It's been such a busy week. That's why I clean forgot to send you your travel notes for Mexico to Beijing. Dave sent me to California, you know. However, it might not be too late, especially as far as the food is concerned.

+ Customs and police: Either a passport or a certified copy of a birth certificate together with a photo is required for entry. Do not forget to apply for a tourist card at the airport. And for Christ's sake, don't argue with cops. Grease their palms. There is no problem a fifty-dollar-note won't solve.
+ Climate and clothing: Mexico City is like spring throughout the year. Business suits for men are appropriate in the cities. By the way, Mexican women are said to be the most beautiful in the world. Buy her a pant suit for the hotel. You can wear your sport shirts and your ridiculous safari shorts for all social occasions in the coastal zones.
+ Health: I know you've got a delicate stomach, so don't eat raw vegetables. They aren't safe. Tap water is usually not drinkable. By the way, they have good doctors and psychiatrists in Mexico City. I'm afraid you will need one.
+ Relationships: I hope you and Dave managed to sort all your problems out. You asked me how I was getting on with Dave. I expect he has already told you that Dave and me had a sort of "love at first sight" thing. I'm sorry about it, James, but I guess I simply need an older man.

Best regards,
Jane

PS. Sorry to tell you this in writing!

🙂 Time for a smile

The softer[1] the currency[2] in a foreign country is, the harder the toilet paper.

---
1 weich 2 Währung

FOCUS ON MEXICO

Epilogue

Today there is a board meeting at SASL. Present are Dr Mayer (**M**), Finances, Lou Grade (**G**), CEO and Jim Dale (**D**), Vice President, Sales and Marketing. Poor old Jamie (**J**) has been invited, too. But where is Dave?

G: ... and so we'd like to thank you for doing a great job on your sales drive. The results were astonishing. Jim, could you give Mr Kelly a summary?

D: Sure thing. Well, basically England, Germany, France, Japan and Mexico, no business. We'll have to discuss reasons for that later. Right on target were Portugal, Russia, Saudi Arabia, China. Smaller contracts in Ireland and Spain. All in all more than 60 percent success.

M: Yes, Mr Kelly, and you can imagine the financial implications, can't you? We're very pleased.

J: We were a good team. Oh, by the way where...?

G: Dave has had to leave us for personal reasons. He's gone without giving proper notice. He took one of our female employees with him. All in all not very reliable. So there's a gap. I'd like you to fill it, my boy. Sales Director. We know you're a bit young, but go for it!

J: Gee, sir, that's very kind of you, but I'll have to think about it.

G: Not much to think about, is there, with an offer like this?

J: Well, sir, I've been offered three other jobs including one as Sales Director of a Saudi subsidiary here in the US. Also a result of my sales drive.

G: Okay. You're obviously a man in demand, with a future. Consider your options and get back to me! That's all for now.

James seems to have a bright future. You know his character and experience. What will he do? Which job, if any, will he take?

Chapter 17

Vocabulary to help you with the text

apple pie; everything's ~	alles in bester Ordnung
appropriate	angemessen
board meeting	Vorstandssitzung
carry weight	Gewicht haben, bedeutend sein
certified copy	beglaubigte Kopie
coastal zone	Küstengebiet
cop	Polizist, Bulle
deposit (v)	hinterlegen, aufbewahren
dime; not worth a ~	keinen Pfennig wert
drive	hier: Elan, Dynamik, Schwung
exclude	ausschließen
fill a gap	eine freie Stelle ausfüllen
gap	Lücke
gear	Ausrüstung
go for	zugreifen, akzeptieren
grease someone's palm	jemanden bestechen
hit the brakes	auf die Bremse treten
implication	Auswirkung, Folgen
meritocracy	Leistungsgesellschaft
mining	Bergbau
notice; give proper ~	fristgerecht kündigen
offending car	hier: Unfallverursacher
confirm in writing	schriftlich bestätigen
pant suit	Hosenanzug
pattern	Struktur, Muster
rear lights	Rücklichter
remove	entfernen, wegnehmen
reverse	rückgängig machen
right on target!	ins Schwarze getroffen!
shoot!	schieß los!
since	hier: da, weil
status-conscious	statusbewußt
subsidiary	Tochtergesellschaft
traffic police	Verkehrspolizei
trunk (BE: boot)	Kofferraum

FOCUS ON MEXICO 17

vein of gold	Goldader
virtue	Tugend
vital documents	lebenswichtige Dokumente
wheels of commerce	Räderwerk des Handels
your hair'll stand on end	die Haare werden dir zu Berge stehen

🙂 Time for a smile

Lou Grade had to write the following letter of excuse for not being able to meet delivery the dates agreed with Spain.

Dear Sir,

Our director, Dave Makeit, has been kidnapped by left-wing guerrillas in Mexico. From what you have told me, your order must have been in Dave's order book at the time he was captured. Negotiations with the guerrillas are at a very delicate stage, but we hope to have Dave – and his order book – out by Christmas.
In the meantime, if we could have a deposit from you, it would help us to meet the kidnapper's financial expectations. It means such a lot to poor Dave's wife and three children.

Yours sincerely,
Lou Grade

Adapted from Ch. Ward, *Our Cheque is in the Post*

KEY TO THE EXERCISES

CHAPTER 1

Task 1: Train your brain
1. What does James sell? — **c** sports aids for the slow learner.
2. What does SASL mean? — **b** sports aids for the slow learner
3. Where is his home-town located? — **b** on the fork of the Mississippi and Minnesota Rivers

Task 2: Understanding the Americans (1)
1. You got it! — **b** That's exactly right.
2. Got ya! — **a** I see what you mean.
3. Piece of cake! — **c** It's as easy as that!
4. Bring back that cabbage. — **c** Fetch those dollars in.

Task 3: Understanding the Americans (2)

A British person says	Our Americans have said
You've done a great job this year.	You did a great job this year.
a group of neighbouring states	a bunch of states stuck together
That's exactly right.	Dead on!
I see what you mean.	Got ya!
It's as easy as that!	Piece of cake!
I think ...	I guess ...
Music's not my cup of tea.	Music is not my thing.
Fetch those dollars in!	Bring in that cabbage!
bloke	dude
my boy	baby
See you!	See ya!

Task 4: Watch their ways
Would German or English people do the following?
Dave: *(pumping James' hand and slapping him on the shoulder).*

Task 5: American manners
Dave and James call each other by their first names. It is like saying *du* to someone in Germany. (It's false. If you are a foreign visitor, most people will probably say to you "Please call me Dave". Neighbours, colleagues, bosses, people you have met at a party are normally called by their first names. Customers usually call the

KEY TO THE EXERCISES

employees of a company by their first names.)
Americans pay each other more compliments than Germans do. (It's true. Most Americans are very generous with compliments and very careful to avoid critical or personal remarks. Say "Thank-you" and accept the compliment).

Only very old-fashioned people will be shocked if you use so-called four letter words like shit, fuck in informal every-day conversation. (It's false again).

James: "Well, *sir*, he's about the same age as you, Dave." In everyday conversation 'sir' is no longer a form of respect. (So it's false).

CHAPTER 2

Task 1: Train your brain
1. this pile of rusting metal. He's referring to **(a)** the aircraft
2. travelling so far from the real world. **(b)** leaving the United States
3. a visit to the oldest democracy. **(c)** a visit to Britain

Task 2: Understanding American English

It's almost as big as the Big Apple.	It's almost as big as New York.
Right on.	You're completely right.
Don't get all shook up!	Don't get offended!
What the hell's cuisine?	What the devil's cuisine?
There're things I'm hooked on.	There're things I like.
They don't pay a cent of tax.	They don't pay a penny of tax.
They've got some McDonald's joints.	You've got some McDonald's outlets (shops).
A double bourbon for my buddy.	A double whisky for my friend.

Task 3: Did you get the hidden message?

They say	They think
1. What's taking you to little cold England, if I might ask?	**b** Why don't you stay where you come from?
2. Excuse me, would you?	**c** Keep your sticky fingers off my knickerbockers.
3. I hope there are other enticements in a visit to the oldest democracy?	**d** You Yanks have no culture. You're only interested in money and shopping.
4. I must remember to turn my watch back five hundred years.	**a** These Europeans are so old-fashioned.

Task 4: American manners
True (T) or False (F)

1. If you are invited to an American home, you should bring flowers for the hostess. (Don't, it's a European custom. Ring them up and ask if you should bring a salad or dessert. If not, bring a box of chocolates or a souvenir from your country.) **F**

2. Americans normally wish each other "Good appetite" before they begin a meal together. (No they don't. They might offer you the bowls and say "Help yourself". Some families hold hands and say a short prayer.) **F**

3. It is considered polite to leave a little bit of food on your plate when you have finished eating. (Don't! Your host might think you don't like the dish and be disappointed. However, in restaurants it is perfectly acceptable to leave food on your plate or even to ask for a doggy box to take home what you can't finish.) **F**

4. Guests in an American home usually offer to help in the kitchen. (Right! It is polite to ask if there is anything you can help with around the house.) **T**

5. You need to go to the toilet? Don't ask "May I use your toilet, please?" (The word toilet sounds unpleasant to American ears. In private homes you say "May I use your bathroom?" In restaurants it is the restroom, the men's room or the ladies' room.) **F**

6. When they ask you "How do you like the USA?" they expect you a frank and honest answer. (No, they don't, so don't mention the negative sides of the country. They expect you to give a short positive answer. This applies not only to the US. If a family is kind enough to invite you, they don't want to hear negative things from the foreign guest). **F**

7. If you feel hot, you may ask if you can open a door or a window, although almost all rooms are air-conditioned. (Yes, you may. In American offices, schools and private homes doors are usually left open. A closed door is the sign that a room is occupied. So leave the door of the bathroom (toilet) open if you're not using it. Other members of the family might be waiting impatiently for someone to come out.) **T**

Task 5: Patch work – Airport English

I'd like to book an early flight from New York to London, please.
Where's the check-in desk, please?
Could I have an aisle seat, please?
Which gate do I depart from?
How many pieces of baggage do you have?
Have you left your luggage unattended at any time?
Excuse me, where is the departure lounge?

KEY TO THE EXERCISES

What are my duty-free allowances?
Flight number 492 to London is now boarding at gate 25.
Would all passengers for flight number LH 432 please proceed to gate 52 immediately.

Task 6: The travelling manager's British country quiz
Part I: People and politics
1. Great Britain consists of England, Wales, Scotland, Northern Ireland.
2. There are three Parliaments in the United Kingdom.
3. In Northern Ireland religion plays an important role.
4. In Britain 35% say they have no religion. That is the highest percentage in Europe after the Netherlands.
5. The UK has a population of about 57 million of which 47 million live in England. **c**
6. London has got 7 million inhabitants. **b**
7. In the centre of London there live the very rich and the very poor. **c**
8. Britain hasn't got a written constitution. **d**
9. The Parliament consists of the House of Lords and the House of Commons. **c**
10. The House of Commons is more powerful.

Part 2: Bosses and workers
1. Thirteen percent of the working population is self-employed. **c**
2. In the UK companies have greater freedom. One reason is that there is almost no worker participation at decision-making levels.
3. The average British person prefers to work in a team with which they can identify. **b**
4. In France and Germany companies spend a lot of money on training their staff. Britain spends 17% of what French and German companies do. **c** At higher levels training is regarded as a reward rather than a preparation for a new job.
5. 45% of the workforce are women. **a**
6. Yes. Women are more often found in managerial positions than in other European countries.
7. A company car allows a manager to avoid taxes. **a**
8. You sign a business letter to a business partner whose name you know with 'yours faithfully'. **a**
9. You sign a business letter to a business partner whose name you don't know 'yours sincerely'. **b**
10. He is not interested in what you have to offer. **a**

CHAPTER 3

Task 1: Train your brain
1. Where does the meeting take place? (**a**) at a golf club
2. What did James order as hors d'oeuvre? (**b**) a shrimp salad
3. What does Mr Johnson eat? **c** fish
4. When and where are they going to talk business? (**a**) at the club-house

Task 2: Understanding American English (1)

British English	American English
You've just got to travel	You just got to travel.
Do you have anything similar?	You got anything like that?
Oh my dear!	God man!
Thanks, no, I'd fancy a coke.	Gosh, no, I need a coke.
I'm beginning to understand this place.	I'm really beginning to get the hang of this country.
It's fantastic.	It's a real trip.

Task 3: Understanding American English (2)

American English	British English
1. French fries	**e** chips
2. cookie	**c** biscuit
3. biscuit	**d** scone
4. surf-and-turf	**a** steak and lobster
5. potato chips	**b** crisps

Task 4: The hidden message

Director Johnson says	Director Johnson thinks
1. You Americans are so clever.	**b** Stupid foreigner!
2. Oh, is that so?	**c** What a silly thing to say!
3. Actually, I've never thought about it.	**a** I would not dream of doing a thing like that.
4. ... will British ketchup be good enough?	**e** You chauvinist Yankee.
5. How interesting!	**d** What a bore you are!

Task 5: Patch work – At the restaurant
A table for two, please.
Have you booked a table, sir?
Could we have that table in the corner?
Waiter, could we have the menu please?
What do you recommend today?

KEY TO THE EXERCISES

Charles, could you take our order, please?
What do you fancy as an apéritif?
And what about an hors d'œuvre?
Could I have a receipt, please?
Do you accept credit cards?

Task 6: Watch their ways

American English	British English
1. Jack'll blow his top.	d Our chairman might disagree.
2. You're talking bullshit.	c I'm not quite with you on that.
3. You gotta be kidding.	b How interesting, however ...
4. I tell you, I can walk away from this deal.	e I'm afraid, we all have to do our homework.
5. Bean-counters drive me mad.	a Accountants can be frustrating.

Task 7 : Country quiz – British manners

1. The English shake hands. **c** It all starts with a handshake.
2. James has an appointment with Mr Johnson. What do you think is most likely to happen? **a** Mr Johnson will stretch out his hand first.
3. How should James introduce himself? **b** I'm James Kelly.
4. A potential customer asks "How do you do?" What is your reaction? **c** "How do you do?"
5. A good business partner arrives. How do you greet him? **a** "How are you, Paul?"
6. A colleague greets you: "How are you, Bob?" How do you react? **b** Fine, thank you.
7. Mr McGregor is not amused because the Scots believe that a foreigner should know that Edinburgh is not in England.

CHAPTER 4

Task 1: Train your brain

1. What does Director Johnson think of James' product?
    c He is not interested because British players are not violent.
2. What is the advantage of the Breakable Simulated Golf Club?
    a It prevents the angry golfer from breaking his club.
3. What do you think? Is the breakable club a real US patent?
    b It is an existing patent.

Task 2: Understanding the Americans (1)

1. The bottom line is ...
2. goodies
3. You're the CEO
4. How does that grab you?
5. Sure!
6. You'll be blown away.
7. Check this out!

f The final result is ...
g interesting, fine products
d You are the managing director.
c What do you think of that?
e Of course!
b You'll be surprised, astonished.
a Have a look at this!

Task 3: Watch their ways

What James says and ...

1. I'll call you later so that we can discuss prices.
2. OK, Coll. Interest you?
3. Where the hell is the waiter?
4. It'll knock your socks off.
5. You're all aces at the sport.
6. I don't like that old stuff. A good coke is all a man needs.

... why he says it

c Americans are impatient, time is money.
e They get on first-name terms quickly.
a They are impatient, time is money.
d They use violent language.
f Americans are generous with compliments.
b American way of life is best.

Task 4: Understanding the Americans (2)

British English	American English
I don't drink that kind of alcohol.	I don't like that old stuff.
I'm certain we'll get on well.	I'm sure we're going to hit it off.
... and there you are!	Wham, bam, thank you, ma'am.
Try harder!	Come on, man!
That's the great advantage.	That's the beauty.

Task 5: Say it the English way

He doesn't say	He says
That is impossible.	I'm afraid that would not be possible.
I like that device.	I quite like this little device.
That's a negative attitude.	That's not a very positive attitude.
I think these figures are wrong.	I beg your pardon, but I'm afraid these figures are not quite right.
We need more money for the project.	I'm afraid we might need a little more money for the project.
We have a cash-flow problem.	I'm afraid we have a slight cash-flow problem.
I have reservations as to this project.	I have some reservations as to the success of this project.
I think that is dangerous.	I'm afraid that might be a bit dangerous.

KEY TO THE EXERCISES

CHAPTER 5

Task 1: Train your brain
1. O'Leary has 60% learners.
2. They are eating Guinness and oysters.
3. James shows him the beeping golf ball.
4. It helps to find the ball.

Task 2: Patchwork – Small talk and business talk
So, let's raise our glasses to our good health.
I really admit that this tastes better after the third or fourth glass.
Can I offer you some oysters with your Guinness?
Guinness and oysters are almost a national dish here in Ireland.
I'll certainly appreciate it, too.
Let's come straight to the point.
And that's where SASL comes in.
I'm sure I've no idea what you're getting at.
Let's take it step by step.
Just give me an overview, no details at this stage.

Task 3: Understanding American English

American English	British English
1. sidewalk	e pavement
2. first floor	d ground floor
3. trunk	c boot
4. trunk call	b long distance call
5. highway	a motorway

Task 4 : The travelling manager's Irish country quiz
1. The Capital of Northern Ireland is Belfast. **b**
2. The Capital of the Republic of Ireland is Dublin. **a**
3. How many people speak German? **c** 2%
4. How many people live in the Republic of Ireland? **a** 4 million
5. In Ireland you have to drive on the left. **c**
6. Who is the greatest investor in Ireland? The USA. **b**
7. With Irish business partners you are quickly on first-name terms. It's true. **a**
8. A typical Irish dish is Guinness with oysters.
9. Murphy's is a well-known porter brewed in Limerick. **c**
10. Who is the patron saint of Ireland? St. Patrick. **a**
11. What second language is spoken in Ireland? Gaelic. **b**
12. What could you not advertise in the media? Tobacco **a** and alcohol. **c**

CHAPTER 6

Task 1: Train your brain
1. James came by Air Lingus.
2. The first forms were only for Lufthansa passengers.
3. The first employee was a student who did not know the regulations.

Task 2: Going International - airport English

Dürfte ich Sie kurz belästigen?	Could I bother you a minute?
Ich habe mich hier verlaufen.	I've got myself lost here.
Können Sie mir sagen, wie ich zur Gepäckausgabe komme?	Could you tell me how I can get to the baggage return?
Folgen Sie einfach den Schildern.	Just follow the signs.
Mein Gepäck ist nicht mitgekommen.	My luggage didn't get here.

Task 3 : Understanding American English (1)

British English	American English
I'll ask this man.	I'll just check it out with this guy.
What a rude fellow!	Jesus, what a creep!
Where's the baggage claim, please?	Where's the baggage return, please?
Excuse me, madam, ...	Gee ma'am, ...
She's just run away.	She just took off.

Task 4: Typical German mistakes

They said	They should have said
You can become a plan at ...	You can get a plan at ...
become: werden, get: bekommen	
I have been last year in Boston	I was in Boston last year.
1. Falsche Zeit. 2. Deutsch: Zeit vor Ort. Englisch: Ort vor Zeit	
Thank you for your kidneys.	Thank you for you kindness.
(Kidneys sind Nieren)	
The airplane arrived one hour ago.	

Task 5 : Understanding American English (2)
AE is tough, exaggerated, sensational. BE is understated, modest, vague, reserved.
By the way, each pair has the same meaning.

Which is which? American English (AE) or British English (BE)?

1 a   Dave will blow his top. **AE**
1 b   Our chairman might tend to disagree. **BE**
2 a   I'm not quite with you on that. **BE**

KEY TO THE EXERCISES

2 b You're talking bullshit. **AE**
3 a That's a beautiful scenario. **AE**
3 b We might find a way of making that work. **BE**
4 a Bean-counters drive me mad. **AE**
4 b Accountants can be a nuisance. **BE**
5 a Will they ever be a force in business again? **BE**
5 b Will they ever come back from the grave? **AE**
6 a You gotta be kidding. **AE**
6 b Hmm, that's an interesting idea. **BE**

Task 6: Our country quiz: Ireland – Britain – Germany
A. How many adults can follow a discussion in a foreign language?
1. 2 % (**c**) of the adult Irish can follow a discussion in German and 12 % (**a**) in French.
2. 6 % **c** of the adult British population have this qualification in German and 15% (**b**) in French.
3. And what about the Germans? English: 43% (**c**) and French: 18% (**c**)
By the way, of all the European nations the Dutch are the best speakers of foreign languages.

B. How strong are their economies?
1. Ireland has the highest and Germany the lowest birthrate.
2. There are only two countries within the European Union where the birth rate is higher than the death rate: Spain and Ireland.
3. By the year 2030 16 % (**b**) will be under 20.
4. Life in Germany can be up to 60% (**a**) more expensive than in Greece.
5. What about their gross national products (1992 in billion $)?
   Ireland: **c** 18,73 – Great Britain: **b** 518, 8 – Germany: **a** 761, 8

CHAPTER 7

Task 1: Train your brain
1. What kind of company is S.U.P.? **a** a software company
2. Dr. Recht means: **c** What a blunt fellow you are.
3. Mr Blitz means: **a** I hope you haven't come unprepared.
4. James means: **b** Our postal service is well organised.
5. **a** In Germany we do business step by step.

Task 2: Cross-cultural awareness test (1)
a We have naturally checked all the data you sent us in detail. **4**
b Of course I got the whole package. You've got a hell of a fine business going here. **5**
c Now straight to the point. **2**

d I'm afraid we haven't got enough time for the history of your company. **2**
e Your beginners won't waste their time searching for balls. **5**

Task 3: Understanding American English

British English	American English
You can be sure I will.	You bet I will.
a whole lot of things	a whole bunch of equipment
make something work well	make something hum
Certainly!	Sure thing!
Sorry gentlemen.	Sorry gents.

Task 4: Cross-cultural awareness test (2)

It reminds me of a funny story about a friend of mine. **1A**
Perhaps I could begin by explaining the tasks of the people present here. **1G**
Let me just give you a short presentation of our company and our product range. **7A**
A presentation of your company? Could we just keep to the subject, if you don't mind? **7G**
What do you think about it, Herr Dr. Recht? **2G**
Hi, everybody. Just call me Jamie. **2A**
Could you explain them one at a time in detail? **3G**
Now let's come to our deal. **6A, 8A**
How many balls are you going to take? My special offer is ... **5A**
Just a moment, please. Could you first tell us more about those computer simulated tests? **6G**

Task 5: The hidden meaning – philosophers test (1)

1. United States   **c** self-reliance   Selbstvertrauen
2. Great Britain   **d** non-conformity   Andersartigkeit
3. Spain   **a** self-centredness   Ichbezogenheit
4. Germany   **b** autonomy   Selbständigkeit

Task 6: The hidden meaning - philosopher's test (2)

1. Italy, France   **d** Smooth social relationships are more important than the truth.
2. Britain   **c** The truth is the truth as long it doesn't rock the boat (create unnecessary problems).
3. Japan   **b** Adherence to the truth must not destroy the harmony and balance of society.
4. China   **a** There is no absolute truth.

Task 7: The travelling manager's country quiz

1. Which is the biggest country in the European Union? France **c**
2. What do Germans understand by individual leadership? Autonomy **b**

KEY TO THE EXERCISES

3. What were the Germans most proud of? Their 'Grundgesetz' 30% **b** (only 17% were proud of our economical achievement).
4. Who dominates Germany's business? The big German banks **a**
5. What is the English for Aufsichtsrat? Supervisory board **c**
6. Which businessmen think that German managers are too slow? Americans and Australians **a**
7. What do other nations think of German advertising? It gives a lot of detailed product information, but it is not visual enough and a bit boring. **b**

CHAPTER 8

Task 1 : Train your brain
1. What does James mean by "You've a wide spread"?
   a You've hotels all over the country.
2. What is special about the mountain bike James has to offer?
   b The hotel can locate and pick up a guest in case of trouble.
3. Why do the Portuguese ask James for support?
   c They are excellent negotiators who know how to keep costs down.

Task 2: Cross-cultural awareness test (1)
Just for your information, we'll make a protocol of what we've discussed today. **7**

J: Where would you like me to begin? M: That's entirely up to you. You are the specialist. **4.2**

Of course we couldn't quite understand ... the advantages which your equipment offers. **4.1**

Oh, one other thing before you leave us. **4.3**

... but do you have something else that would help Sporty-Rest to stand out from the rest? **5**

Task 3: Cross-cultural awareness test (2)
Sorry to interrupt you, but I'm afraid we haven't got enough time for the history of your company. Let's keep to the subject. **G**

Well, perhaps you could give us a brief overview of what you consider might be most useful and successful here in our environment? **P**

I quite like that little device, however I'm not absolutely sure that this type of instrument will be of any use to our clients. **E**

We've got a whole bunch of equipment which could make your company hum. You'll hum so much you'll be able to light up a football stadium. **A**

Task 4 : Patch work
We've spent some time reading your documentation about your very interesting products.

We're certainly excited to hear what you have to tell us.

I must apologise for being late, but it has been one of those days.

And we would hope that you would support us with the publicity

As for my humble self I'm responsible for purchasing.

I see you've done your homework.

Perhaps you could give us a brief overview of what you consider might be most useful here in our environment?

If we have understood your excellently illustrated documentation correctly ...

Oh no, Mr Kelly, that's perfectly all right.

If you'll excuse me please, I'll be back in a minute.

CHAPTER 9

Task 1: Train your brain
1. James' surfboard is equipped with a small motor and a compass. **b**
2. The rod is equipped with a device to shoot the line. **c**
3. Pedro is making "an exception". He is ready to talk business in a restaurant. **a**

Task 2: Cross-cultural awareness test (1)
1. Yes, I was over on the other side of your peninsula, in Portugal. Beautiful country. *(It's not the Spanish but the Iberian Peninsula.)*
2. Well, heck no! I just love your rosé wine. I'll take a ..., what's its name? Ah, yes, Mateus Rosé? *(Mateus Rosé is a Portuguese wine)*
3. I think I would suggest Paella before you choose something Portuguese. *(It shows a certain dislike of the Portuguese.)*
   P: ... unfortunately history hasn't granted us ownership of that charming place yet. *(He thinks the Iberian Peninsula should belong to Spain.)*
4. They are rarely on time. And they often deal with several tasks at a time.
5. In Portugal people are addressed by their christian names. Manuel da Fonsa is Senhor Manuel. But in Spain and Spanish speaking countries, the last name is the main one. Pedro Barca is Señor Barca. A person senior to you may address you by your first name. Don't follow his example unless specifically invited. Unmarried women are addressed as Señorita plus first name. So James got it right this time.

Task 3: Pitfalls for marketing managers (1)
Parker Pens' slogan: 'Prevent embarrassment - use Parker Ink' came across like a birth control ad in Latin America where the Spanish word used in for embarrassment, *emberazo*, actually means pregnancy.

No va means "it doesn't go" which is unsuitable for a car.

KEY TO THE EXERCISES

Task 4: Cross-cultural awareness test (2)

Title of article	Nationality
1. How to breed bigger and better elephants	**d** American
2. The origin and development of the Indian elephant in the years 1200 - 1978	**c** German
3. The love life of elephants in central Africa	**b** French
4. How we sent an elephant to the moon	**f** Russian
5. Hunting Elephants in East Africa	**a** English
6. Techniques of elephant fighting	**e** Spanish

Task 5: Pitfalls for marketing managers (2)

1. In Spanish *fiera* means 'ugly old woman'. (Source: L. Copeland & L.Griggs)
2. Just in time someone remembered that in Mexican-Spanish *caliente* is the slang word for 'street-walker'.

Task 6: Cross-cultural awareness test (3.

The German (G); The Spanish (S)

works fixed hours	G	changes plans if necessary	S
is impatient	S	is extrovert	S
brief on the phone	G	separates job and private life	G
rarely writes memos	S	works step by step	G
contacts top key persons	S	works any hours	S
argues logically	G	contacts head of department	G

Task 7: The travelling manager's country quiz

1. Salaries of top managers differ considerably in Europe.

Country (1992)	Salary in pounds/year
1 Britain	**f** 87,000
2 France	**b** 98,000
3 Italy	**d** 105,000
4 Germany	**a** 110,000
5 Switzerland	**e** 123,000
6 Spain	**c** 125,000

2. Spaniards have gone to the polls more than 50 times (**b**) since the referendum in 1976.

3. Who are these letters addressed to?

   a *Muy Sr. mío* – to a Spanish male person
   b *Esmo Senhor Rodrigo* – to a Portuguese

4. Spaniards spend 37% of their money on furniture, carpets etc.; 13% on electrical household equipment and 28 % on services.
5. Extranjeros are foreigners (**c**). The Basques live in France and Spain. Where they came from is unknown. Their language is not a European one. **b**
6. The Spanish drink more beer than wine.
7. The Spanish treat them with respect and dignity. **b**

CHAPTER 10

Task 1 : Train your brain
1. What is the meeting about?
> **c** They are discussing the quotation of SASL.

2. What is a T.S.U.?
> **b** It is a racket that gives acoustic and tactile signals to correct the body position and the swing of the player.

3. Why do they disagree about the price?
> **a** and **b** SASL's quotation and James' price per unit do not correspond. The new improved version 1.3. is more expensive than version 1.1.

Task 2: Cross-cultural awareness test

Mon dieu! Monsieur Kelly, has anything gone wrong?	3
.. or, as Descartes would have put it, Cogi ...	9
Since Mr Kelly hasn't been able to bring his interpreter, we'll have to conduct the meeting in English for a change.	5
Monsieur Kelly, we've been expecting you.	2
My name's Kratzenberg. I'm the president of this establishment. On my right is Mr Gordois, our director of sport, and to his right you see Mrs Schleicher, my assistant.	4
Ah, my young friend, what does an American know of le savoir-vivre?	8
I'm sure, Mr Kelly, that France has no more and no fewer lazy or untalented people than any other ... hmm ... civilized country.	8
I beg your pardon, Mr Kelly, but in your documentation you quoted us a figure of 155 dollars per system.	6
I think we should put the linguistic question on the agenda of our next staff meeting where we will have to find a French brandname for the thing.	7

KEY TO THE EXERCISES

Task 3: Patchwork – Words chairmen will use

It's my great pleasure to introduce Mr James Kelly to you.

Mr Kelly, may I present our little team to you?

We'll have to conduct the meeting in English for a change.

And now I'd like to declare this meeting open.

My assistant will take the minutes of this meeting for later reference.

Mr Gordois will give us a résumé of the situation up to now.

Mr Gordois would you like to comment on this?

I think we should put the linguistic question on the agenda of our next staff meeting.

Thank-you for your contribution, Mrs Schleicher.

We will continue with our discussions after the meal.

Task 4: Understanding more American English

British English	American English
1. We've bought the *block of flats*.	e I'd have preferred an *apartment house*.
2. It's at the big *crossroads*.	c I thought it was at an *intersection*.
3. Paul's office is on the *first floor*.	f And I thought your office was on the *second floor*.
4. My office is on the *ground floor*.	a I thought it was on the *first floor*.
5. I'll arrive on *12/4/1998*.	b We expected you 4/12/1998.
6. The *4/12/1998* will be fine.	d The *12/4/1998* will be too early.

Task 5: The travelling manager's country quiz

1. France is the least densely populated European country. **a** Most people live in the big cities. You would find a construction site in the middle of nowhere at a reasonable price.

2. Which three countries have the same number of inhabitants? **a** Denmark, **b** Belgium and **e** Portugal have about ten million inhabitants.

3. In France. **a** Humour is used neither to break the ice nor to warm up the audience. So do not sprinkle your presentation with jokes because business is a serious matter.

4. In which country is it most difficult to settle disagreement by compromise? **a** The French see the meeting as a forum for their own cleverness. Cold logic leads to the only possible conclusion. That is why they refuse to make concessions or to compromise.

5. How much is VAT on advertising in the French media? **b** 18.6 %

6. The question is a difficult one. Don't worry if you got it wrong.

Eurosports BV : Besloten Vennootschap (GmbH), Netherlands
Topgolf SpA : Società per Azioni (AG), Italy
Unisports SA : Société anonyme (GmbH), France
Allrounders Lda : Sociedade por Quotas de Resposibilidade Limitada (GmbH), Portugal.

CHAPTER 11

Task 1 : Train your brain

1. Russians negotiate like chess players. They think several moves ahead.

2. Russians make concessions on some minor matters to get bigger concessions from you.

3. They don't feel comfortable if you drop new ideas because they would have to go to their boss to ask for his okay.

4. Sam advises James not to compromise. Russians would regard it as sign of weakness.

5. What do you do when they present you with a draft of a contract? Often Russian negotiators come to the meeting with an initial draft outlining their position. However, it's not their final position. Don't take it too seriously.

6. Contracts are often made of "rubber". They stick to them as long as things are going well. They'll bend them as soon as things go wrong.

7. Three ways of building bridges:
   1) Open up your heart, tell them about your hopes and problems.
   2) Talk about your family. Show them photos.
   3) Do business in saunas and in restaurants.

Task 2: Understanding American English

British English	American English
What a thin-looking piece of chicken!	What a scraggy looking piece of chicken!
I thought things had improved.	I thought things had gotten better.
You can be sure about that.	You bet!
Don't get nervous!	Don't sweat it!
I certainly can.	Sure can.
It's nothing special.	No big deal.

Task 3: True (T) or False (F)

1. They use tough talk if they feel in a stronger position. **T**
2. Bluntness wins friends both in Detroit and in Kiev. **T**

KEY TO THE EXERCISES

3. Keep smiling when meeting them in meetings. **F**
4. A contract is binding as long as both sides profit by it. **T**
5. Personal relationships are more important than money. **T**
6. Russians are neither title nor status-conscious. **F**
7. They negotiate step by step, like Germans and Americans. **F**
8. Excessive profit margins are looked on as illegitimate. **T**

Task 4: How do different nations view contracts?
France 1, Italy 2, Portugal 3, Japan 4, Russia 5
A contract is binding and must be fulfilled. **1, 3**
A contract is a statement of intent and will be reworked when necessary. **4**
A contract that is fulfilled six months later than agreed is better than no contract at all. **2**
A contract is binding as long as both sides profit by it. **5**

Task 5: The travelling manager's country quiz
1. The Russian Federation is (**a**) twice as big as the United States and (**b**) 30 times bigger than France.
2. The Russian Federation covers (**c**) 11 time zones.
3. With 150 million people Russia has less than half of the population of the European Union. **a**
4. 75 % of the population live in cities. **b**
5. About 75% of the state owned businesses have been privatised. **a**
6. Russia has been communist for about 80 years. **c**

CHAPTER 12

Task 1 : Train your brain
1. Mr Ibn Ben Saadi is responsible for the recreation facilities in Saudi Arabia.
2. Dave has joined James because he did not want to leave the negotiations in the hands of junior management.
3. Mrs Rubinstein is a specialist in Islamic law and is supposed to help finalize the contract.
4. Ibn Ben Saadi is interested in the balls because officers and soldiers lose hundreds of balls in the sand dunes.
5. He was not interested in the golf clubs in the first place because they have many grass courts in Saudi.
6. James managed to sell the clubs because he discovered that the collapsible clubs fitted perfectly into the soldiers' combat packs.

Task 2 : Pitfalls for managers

What Mrs Hayman did not know was that you cannot leave the country without an exit visa plus the permission of Saudi sponsor.

Task 3: Mind your manners

1. Dave has brought a female secretary. Arabs prefer to discuss business with men. What is more, Mrs. Rubinstein seems to be Jewish. Jews are not very popular in Arabia, particulary not when they dare to be specialists in Islamic law.
2. Do not call them Mohammedans; they are Moslems.
3. Don't refer to the Gulf as the Persian Gulf. It is the Arab Gulf. The Iranians (Persians) are their enemies.
4. Don't discuss women, don't refer to parts of their body (their delicate legs).

Task 4 : Watch their ways

What is typical (T) and what is untypical (U) of the Arab manager?
1. He arrives for the meeting on time. **U**
2. He speaks in a loud voice. **T**
3. He expects you to ask if his family is well. **T**
4. Home is private. He does not invite foreigners to his house. **U**
5. He will stand close to you, touch you and keep eye contact. **T**
6. He will keep his sunglasses on when talking to you. **U**
7. He talks a lot and in a loud voice. It is a sign of strength. **T**
8. Qualified secretaries guarantee that your meeting will not be disturbed by phone calls or visitors. **U**
9. If he accepts you as a friend you can no longer refuse his requests, nor can he yours. **T**

Task 5: The travelling manager's country quiz

1. Shops are closed on Friday **c** because it is a holy day (in some Arab countries also on Sunday). **a**
2. North Vietnam is The People's Republic of Vietnam.
   Mainland China or Red China is The People's Republic of China (when you are in China).
   The Persian Gulf is the Arab Gulf when you are in Saudi Arabia.
   Taiwan is The Province of Taiwan for mainland Chinese.
3. Arabs consider it offensive when you show the sole of your foot. **c** Pointing with your finger is impolite in Japan. Eating with your fingers is OK in Arab countries.
4. How do you eat in Saudi Arabia? **a** Using your right hand.

KEY TO THE EXERCISES

5. Avoid discussing religion in Saudi Arabia and don't call them Mohammedans - they are Moslems. **b**
6. There are 21 Arab states. **b**
7. About 200 million people live in these states. **b**
8. The capital of Saudi Arabia is Riyadh. **b**

CHAPTER 13

Task 1: Train your brain
1. Japanese do not change companies every two or three years. Most of them stay with their company for a life-time. It is almost like a family.
2. The company comes first. It is more important than the individual's name who identifies with it: Sonya Sports, Marketing Manager, Kenichi Yamasaki.
3. The girl addressed James as Mr SASL because on his card the name comes after the name of the company. In Japan the company name comes first.

Task 2: Match the English against the Japanese
1. beer   **c** beelu
2. radio   **e** ladio
3. salary   **a** sarali
4. enormous   **b** ah-no-lo-moo-su
5. hostess   **d** hosu-tesu

Task 3: Pitfalls for marketing managers
1. Translated into Japanese Cortina means 'Broken down old car'.
2. What Pan Am didn't know was the fact that in Japan only prostitutes recline.
3. The colour green for computers would be unthinkable in the USA or Germany. However, green is a high-tech colour in Japan.
4. The number 4 is an unlucky number in Japan just as 13 is in Germany and the USA.
5. In western countries the fox is associated with intelligence and cleverness. In Japan, however, it is associated with witches.

Task 4: The travelling manager's country quiz
1. The success of a partnership with a well-established Japanese company is directly related to the strength of inter-personal relationships. **c**
2. Established Japanese companies prefer doing business on the basis of long-term partnerships. **a**
3. You prepare the first meeting through a local agent who knows the executives personally. **b**
4. Don't forget to bring a lot of business cards, 150 would be enough. **c**
5. Have them translated into German, English and Japanese and checked by two experienced Japanese translators. **c**
6. Lee Iacocca earned 20 million dollars a year at Chrysler. **b**

7. Japanese top-managers at a comparable company would earn 10 to 30 times more than his lowest worker. **a**
8. If you want to succeed in Japan you had better change your products and services. Adapt them to your new customer. **b**

CHAPTER 14

Task 1: Train your brain
SASL was founded eight years ago.
James has been working for Dave for more than two years.
Clubs and balls have been adapted to the average size of the Japanese?

Task 2: Watch their ways
1. He put Mr Yamasaki's card into his pocket instead of holding it in two hands and reading it carefully.
2. Mr Yamasaki takes James' card and frowns. Obviously it had not been translated into Japanese. This is a sign of lack of respect.
3. James pumped their hands powerfully. Japanese do not shake hands naturally. If they offer handshakes to westerners it should be followed by a slight bow of you head. The grip should be gentle.
4. James should not have mentioned that his company is only eight years old and that he intends to leave. Japanese are interested in long-established companies and in personal relationships.

Task 3: More pitfalls for marketing managers
1. The executive's office is strictly for work and family snapshots are kept at home in an album.
2. The Japanese salesmen were not interested in the bonus. They are group-orientated and the prize was offered to one of them only. Everyone else would be losers. Not only that: Japanese like to travel, but not with their wives. (source: Copeland and Griggs *Going International*)
3. Nothing had gone wrong. Silence is a sign of respect and closed eyes a sign of concentrated listening.

Task 4: The travelling manager's country quiz
1. BMW and Mercedes are in a well-defined, up-market segment.
   Their cars are status symbols. **b**
2. NEC launches a new product every two or three months.
   They pursue dozens of different projects at a time. **b**
3. Japanese marketing techniques have found a lot of imitators in the world.
   They have not only adopted the strategies but also the vocabulary.
   1 b kaizen: quality control;
   2 c JIt: Just in time;
   3 d zaitech: financial engineering.

KEY TO THE EXERCISES

The aim of JIT is to adapt production output as closely as possible to market demand to reduce costs of storage and avoid waste of man hours. It starts with long-term planning and ends when the product arrives at the customer. Kaizen means total quality control at all stages of production in order to eliminate defects and waste of material.

4. Volkswagen and Nissan don't want to invest in distribution systems. **b**
5. First they buy farms in the USA and then they buy the beef from their own companies. **c**
6. Don't bring your lawyers. **c** Japanese business partners might be offended because it could indicate that you are suspicious. Whatever is discussed and agreed is considered as binding. The written contract is merely a formality. This is reflected by the following figures. In Japan there is only one lawyer for 9000 inhabitants. In the United Kingdom there is one for 800 inhabitants and in the USA there is one per 350 inhabitants.
7. 'Hai' is a polite signal that they are listening attentively to what you are saying **a**. When Japanese say 'Yes' or 'I understand' they merely want to encourrage the speaker.
8. You should know a few more words of Japanese .
   1 Good day   c   kon-nichi wa'
   2 Good bye   d   sayonara
   3 Good evening   a   komban wa'
   4 Please   b   onegai
9. These Japanese companies employ 100,000 people. **a**

CHAPTER 15

Task 1: Train your brain cross-culturally
James did not observe the following commandments: 1, 3, 7, 9, 10

Task 2 : President Reagan's mistake
Tipping is officially not allowed in the People's Republic. The shopkeeper was afraid of getting into trouble.

Task 3: The manager's key to the Great Wall
1. Wait. **b**. It can take months until Chinese get permission to go abroad.
2. Have you sent them an official invitation in writing? **b**.
3. Don't go! **b**. Your Chinese partners have been through a lot of red tape by now (visa, currency etc.). They are looking forward to the rare occasion of going abroad and would be very angry if you spoilt this unique opportunity to see the world. Only a few Chinese are allowed to travel to western countries once in a life-time. Don't make them lose face.
4. You will have to deal with specially-trained negotiators and experts. **a**.

5. The highest-ranking executive is not always the boss. **b** or **c**. Age, experience, contacts (and the rank in the communist party) often count more. Decisions are sometimes taken behind the scenes.
6. Superstition is still a factor to take into account. **c** Buddhists think that spirits from Heaven and Hell return to earth. Therefore they put off important decisions. **a** Avoid the last week of January and the first week of February. They celebrate their New-Moon-Year Feast. Nobody would be willing to talk business with you. **c**

CHAPTER 16

Task 1: Train your brain
1. James pressed the wrong button on his wrist-band and/or there was something wrong with the electronics.
2. Mr Lin Yu Tang said, "Mr Kelly, I have no words" because he was impressed by the singing golf ball.
3. James went pale because the deal would involve a lot of extra services from his company and a lot of extra turnover.
4. He mentioned the gigantic number of potential customers in China in order to get the lowest possible price.

Task 2: Watch their ways
You might have found the following typical ways of negotiating, get the numbers 9, 12, 13, 15.

Task 3: Patchwork - Words negotiators will use
1. Excuse me gentlemen, but I was expecting to meet Mr Lee and his colleagues.
2. We beg you not to trouble yourself about this situation.
3. We are here to learn more about the products.
4. I can certainly fill you in on what we've worked out for you.
5. Now your singing golf-ball is specially customised for you.
6. We would hope for long-term business with your company.
7. We would ask you to take into account the matter of number.
8. The Peoples' Republic is your largest potential market.
9. If we take up business with you, it may be as much as you do with the rest of the world.
10. These things are part of your service, are they not?

Task 4: The manager's key to the Great Wall
1. Don't bring your lawyers. **c** They would think that you do not trust them. The same holds true in Japan. A contract is an agreement between gentlemen. Personal relations are more important than contracts.
2. Modesty is really a weapon in negotiations. **a**

KEY TO THE EXERCISES

3. It is Mr Lin. **b**
4. You'd better shake hands if you don't know the difference between a Chinese, Japanese and Indian bow. **a**
5. With cigarettes and a bottle of fine old whisky you are on the safe side. **a** He wouldn't be able to appreciate the expensive fountain pen because he wouldn't know its price. For the Chinese the feet are the least attractive part of the body. He wouldn't like the idea of wearing the flags of your two countries on his feet. President Bush made precisely this mistake. China's newspapers were indignant.
6. The Chinese are patriots no matter where in the world they live. **a** They see themselves as one big cultural community rather than one nation.
7. The main reason why Chinese officials prefer to do business with big, well-known companies is a question of prestige. If you do business with a small unknown company you might lose face. **c**
8. Well, if there is no lady among your business partners they might see no harm in dating this waitress. **b** Hao shi is a wide-spread custom among business partners in China. Some American companies hire experienced call-girls in case there is no suitable night club in the area. The Chinese businessman expects it, although he is too shy or too modest to ask for it.
9. Dropping your chop sticks is a good omen. **b** You will be invited a second time.

CHAPTER 17

Task1: Train your brain

1. Why was Dave willing to see James Mexico City? He was in California anyway and wanted to discuss a few points with James. **b and c**
2. How did the car accident happen? James did not want to knock a cow over. That is why a truck crashed into his car. **a and b**
3. What reasons did the police give for confiscating the car? They did not accept the photocopies of the car papers. Dave had deposited all his documents at the bank. **a and b**
4. James might have spared himself all the trouble if he had slipped a fifty dollar note between the copies of his documents.
5. Dave did not want to discuss his love affair with James' girl friend on the phone.

Task 2: Pitfalls for managers

The people of the Andes, like many other Third World people, are not used to living according to the whistle of the factory. They like to organise their time themselves. They care more about their time off than about money. When the American company also switched to an hourly basis they were able to hire workers.

KEY TO THE CROSSWORD PUZZLES

Page 22

				¹F	R	²A	N	³C	E		⁴S
	⁵Y		⁶U	E		I		H			L
⁷H	A	C	K	E	D		D	I			A
U				E				⁸P	U	⁹M	P
¹⁰G	A	¹¹T	H	E	R	S				I	
		E		A			¹²T	¹³H	I	N	G
	¹⁴S	A	¹⁵M	P	L	E		A		N	
	H		O			¹⁶Y	A	N	K	E	E
¹⁷L	A	D	S					D		S	
	K		¹⁸S	E	N	D				O	
	E					¹⁹L	O	O	T		
									A		

Page 34

			¹D	E	P	²A	R	³T	U	⁴R	E	
⁵N			O			T		O		O		
⁶A	I	S	L	E		T				L		
T			L				⁷A	P	P	L	E	
I			A							I		
V		⁸P	R	⁹O	C	E	E	D		N		
E		I		N						G		¹⁰J
		L			¹¹B							O
¹²H	¹³E	N	¹⁴C	O	U	N	T	E	R			I
O			H		D							N
¹⁵S	H	A	K	E		¹⁶D	E	T	R	¹⁷O	I	T
T			C			Y				W		
	¹⁸B	O	O	K			¹⁹L	O	U	N	G	E

KEY TO THE CROSSWORD PUZZLES

Page 48

¹C	E	L	L	P	H	O	N	E		²H	A	N	³G
O										O			A
⁴R	O	⁵H	W	⁶O	L	⁷T				S			T
N		O		F		⁸A	C	⁹C	E	P	T		E
E		S				K		H		I		¹⁰B	
R		T				E		I		¹¹T	O	O	L
	¹²M	E	N	U				P		A		A	
		S						S		L		R	
¹³B	O	S	E	¹⁴W	I	T	Z			I		D	
A				E				¹⁵G	E	T		I	
C		¹⁶W	A	L	E	S		I		Y		N	
K				S				F				G	
	¹⁷F	I	S	H		¹⁸P	U	T					

Page 60

¹R	E	²C	E	I	P	³T		⁴F				
		E				E		I		⁵G	A	S⁶
	⁷S	O	⁸H	O		M	A	T	¹⁰T	E	R	O
		H		I		P			H		E	F
		A		T		¹¹D	E	S	T	R	O	Y	T
¹²O	F	F				R			O			E
	T		¹³S	T	E	A	M		U		¹⁴P	I	N
¹⁵K			T			M			G		R	
I		¹⁶D	R	I	V	E			H		¹⁷A	D	¹⁸D
S			I			N					I		E
¹⁹S	²⁰O	C	K	S		T		²¹L			S		L
	N		E		²²O	A	K	E	N		E		A
						L		T					Y

233

Page 72

		[1]B	O	O	T				[2]K		[3]A	
		E					[4]P		[5]I	N	T	O
	[6]S	T	[7]A	R	[8]T	E	R		S			
	I		C		R		[9]O	Y	S	[10]T	E	[11]R
	D		T		U		B			O		A
	E		I		N		L			P		N
	W		V		K		E		[12]M			K
	A		A			[13]U	M	S	A	T	Z	
	L		T						C			
	[14]K	[15]L	E	I	N	S	[16]C	H	R	O	T	H
		I					O		O			
		K		[17]S	O	C	K	S				
[18]B	E	E	P				E					

Page 84

				[1]T							[2]G
	[3]R	O	W	O	H	L	T		[4]F		U
	I			P					O		E
	[5]G	E	T		[6]F	I	[7]G	U	R	E	S
	H				I		A		M		S
	[8]T	[9]O	W	E	L		E				
[10]P		Y			L		[11]L	O	S	T	
[12]R	U	S	H				I				
O		T		[13]B			[14]C	[15]R	E	E	[16]P
[17]B	E	E	P	E	R			A			E
L		R		T				[18]I	N		A
E								S			K
[19]M	A	J	O	R				E			

KEY TO THE CROSSWORD PUZZLES

Page 122

Page 148

GLOSSARY

a rolling stone gathers no moss wer rastet, der rostet
above; the ~ table die obige Tabelle
academic Akademiker
accompany begleiten
account; this ~ s for dies ist eine Erklärung für
accountant Buchhalter
accounting system Buchhaltungssystem
accumulate ansammeln
achieve emotional release Gefühle abreagieren können
achieve a result ein Ergebnis erzielen
achieve a goal ein Ziel erreichen
activate auslösen
actuator Auslöser
add hinzufügen
adherence to the truth Festhalten an der Wahrheit
adjust sich anpassen
administrator Verwalter
admire bewundern
admit zugeben
adopt a strategy eine Strategie übernehmen
adopted theories übernommene Theorien
advantage Vorteil
advertising campaign Werbefeldzug
advice Rat, Ratschlag
affect beeinträchtigen, beeinflussen
aggression builds up Aggressionen stauen sich auf

aid Hilfe
aim Ziel
aircraft engines Triebwerke
aisle seat Sitz im Gang
allocate responsibility Verantwortung zuweisen
allusion Anspielung
Alsatian specialities elsässische Spezialitäten
ambition Ehrgeiz
antipathy Abneigung
apologise sich entschuldigen
apple pie; everything's ~ alles in bester Ordnung
appointment Termin, Verabredung
appreciate mögen, schätzen
approach; the ~ to do sth. die Art, etwas anzupacken
appropriate forum angemessene Platform
appropriate angemessen
approximate requirements ungefähre Anforderungen
arrow Pfeil
artificial leg künstliches Bein; Prothese
astride; sit ~ a horse hoch zu Roß sitzen
at this stage zu diesem Zeitpunkt
attend to someone's needs sich um jemandes Bedürfnisse kümmern
attention span Aufmerksamkeitsspanne

attitude Einstellung, Haltung
average Durchschnitt(s-)
average height durchschnittliche Größe
average; ~ American Durchschnittsamerikaner
avoid vermeiden
avoid misunderstandings Mißverständnisse vermeiden
aware; be ~ of something sich einer Sache bewußt sein

backfire nach hinten losgehen
bargaining Feilschen, Handeln
be into something scharf sein auf, mögen
bean-counters Erbsenzähler
beat around the bush auf den Busch klopfen
beef Rindfleisch
beeper Piepser
beggar Bettler
behaviour Verhalten, Benehmen
Beijing Peking
beneath unterhalb
benefit profitieren, gewinnen
bet one's bottom dollar seinen letzten Pfennig wetten
bill Rechnung
bill someone jemandem etwas in Rechnung stellen

GLOSSARY

blood pressure Blutdruck
bloodless war unblutiger Krieg
blow one's top die Beherrschung verlieren
blunt ungehobelt; direkt, offen
bluntness Direktheit, Grobheit, schonungslose Offenheit
board meeting Vorstandssitzung
bonus system Prämiensystem
book a flight einen Flug buchen
border region Grenzgebiet
bore (n; v) Langweiler; langweilen
boring langweilig
bottom line; and the ~ is und das Resultat ist …
bound; problems are ~ to arise Probleme müssen auftreten
bow sich verbeugen
box of goodies Schachtel mit Bonbons
brain Gehirn
brandname Markenname
brash ungestüm, aufdringlich
break (broke, broken) down eine Panne haben
break off negotiations Verhandlungen abbrechen
breathe atmen
bred; be ~ aufwachsen
breed züchten
bribe (v; n) bestechen; Bestechungsgeld

brief overview kurzer Überblick
brief Anweisungen
briefcase Aktenkoffer
briefing Informationsveranstaltung
brim with self-confidence vor Selbstbewußtsein überschäumen
brothel Bordell
brother-in-law Schwager
brusque brüsk, barsch, schroff
buddy (AE) Kumpel, Kamerad
build bridges Brücken bauen
built-in eingebaut
bullfighting Stierkampf
bullshit Scheißdreck
bully Schläger, Tyrann
bunch; a strange ~ ein sonderbarer Haufen
button Knopf

cabbage Kohl (hier: Dollars, Moneten)
capacity Fähigkeit
carry weight Gewicht haben, bedeutend sein
casual trousers lässige Hosen, Freizeithosen

cater for beliefern, bedienen
cause an emotional drive emotionalen Drang auslösen
cautious vorsichtig
CEO (Chief Executive Officer) Direktor
certified copy beglaubigte Kopie
chambermaid Zimmermädchen
character Person; Charakter
chat plaudern
check this out! passen Sie mal auf!
chip; a ~ off the old block wie der Vater so der Sohn
choose, chose, chosen (aus)wählen
chop sticks Eßstäbchen
chum-up with someone sich mit jemandem anfreunden
clarity; for the sake of ~ um der Klarheit willen
coastal zone Küstengebiet
coincidence Zufall
collapse zusammenbrechen
collect information Informationen sammeln
combat pack Sturmgepäck
come in handy gelegen kommen
comment (n.) Kommentar
comparable vergleichbar
compare vergleichen
comparison Vergleich
competition

GLOSSARY

Wettbewerb
competitor Rivale, Konkurrent
complain sich beschweren, beklagen
complaint Beschwerde, Reklamation
conceal verbergen
concept Vorstellung, Auffassung, Idee
concern Sorge, Angelegenheit
concerning prices was die Preise betrifft
conclude schließen, folgern
conclusion Schlußfolgerung
conduct meetings Besprechungen leiten
confidence Vertrauen, Zutrauen
confirm in writing schriftlich bestätigen
conquer erobern
consider betrachten, halten für
consider things die Dinge überdenken betrachten; erwägen
considerably beträchtlich
considering in Anbetracht
consist of bestehen aus
constitution Verfassung
contain an enemy einen Feind im Zaum halten
contempt Verachtung
continue fortfahren
contradiction Widerspruch

contrary to im Gegensatz zu
controversial strittig
conventional in appearance normal aussehend
convince überzeugen
cookie Keks
cop Polizist, Bulle
correspond entsprechen
courage Mut
courtyard Hof
cover umfassen, bedecken
cowardly feige
cowardly act feige Handlung
crack; a hard nut to ~ eine harte Nuß knacken
crisps Chips
cross-purposes; be at ~ aneinander vorbeireden
cuisine Küche, Gastronomie
current deal das laufende Geschäft
custom Brauch, Sitte
customary üblich
customised maßgeschneidert
customs official Zollbeamter

damn verurteilen
daunting; sound ~ entmutigend klingen
deadlock toter Punkt, Pattsituation
deal Geschäft
decade; it'll take ~s das dauert Jahrzehnte

decision-maker Entscheidungsträger
deck-chair Liegestuhl
declare war on someone jemandem den Krieg erklären
deduct from the taxes von den Steuern absetzen
defeat the enemy den Feind besiegen
delay (v; n) verzögern; Verzögerung
deliberate beraten
deliberately constructed to break bewußt so konstruiert, daß er abknicken muß
delicate legs zarte Beine
delicious köstlich
departure Abschied, Abreise
depend on abhängig sein von
depend on eye contact sich auf Blickkontakt verlassen
deposit (v) hinterlegen, aufbewahren
describe beschreiben
describe the situation die Lage schildern
desert Wüste
desire (n.;v.) Verlangen, Wunsch; begehren
desk Schreibtisch
desperate verzweifelt
destroy zerstören
device Gerät
devoted; be ~ to sich widmen, hingeben
dextrous geschickt, fingerfertig
differentiate unterscheiden
dignity Würde

dime; not worth a ~
keinen Pfennig wert
diplomacy Diplomatie
directly related to direkt
bezogen auf
disease Krankheit
disgrace; in ~
in Ungnade
dishonest unehrlich
dislike of rigid systems
Abneigung gegen
starre Systeme
distance Abstand,
Entfernung
distinguishing mark
herausragendes
Merkmal
distribute verteilen
distribution of the population Verteilung der
Bevölkerung
disturb the peace
den Frieden stören
don't get all shook up
seien Sie nicht gleich
beleidigt
don't let the flies breed on you schlage keine
Wurzeln
dour mürrisch, stur
drain Abfluß
drive hier: Elan,
Dynamik, Schwung
drop new ideas all over the place mit neuen
Ideen um sich werfen
drop a bombshell eine
Bombe platzen lassen
dude Bursche, Kerl
dumbfounded verblüfft
dump versenken

ear plugs Ohrstöpsel
(Ohropax)
ear; I'm all ears
ich bin ganz Ohr
ease Leichtigkeit
elderly; ~ millionaire
älterer Millionär
embarrassed verlegen
emergency Notfall
employment visa
Arbeitsvisum
encounters
Begegnungen
enjoy
mögen, genießen
enterprise
Unternehmen, Firma
entertain unterhalten,
bewirten
entertainment Unterhaltung, Bewirtung
enticements Anreize
environment Gegend,
Milieu; Umgebung
equipped with
ausgestattet mit
escalator Rolltreppe
establishment Firma,
Unternehmen
estimate; rough ~
grobe Schätzung
everybody to his own
jedem das Seine
exaggerate
übertreiben
exaggeration
Übertreibung
exception Ausnahme
exclude ausschließen
execute instructions Anweisungen ausführen
executive leitender
Angestellter

exit visa Ausreisevisum
expensive teuer
experience Erfahrung
facilities Anlagen,
Einrichtungen

familiar; be ~ with
vertraut sein mit
famous berühmt
fancy mögen
fashionable modisch,
modern, elegant
favourite subject
Lieblingsthema
feature Eigenschaft,
Merkmal
fed; be ~ up with die
Nase voll haben von
federal system bundesstaatliches System
federal state
Bundesstaat
feel bound sich verpflichtet fühlen
feel out of place sich
deplaziert fühlen
fill someone in on
jemanden informieren
über
fill a gap eine freie
Stelle ausfüllen
finalise a contract
einen Vertrag zum
Abschluß bringen
financial implications
finanzielle
Auswirkungen
findings Ergebnisse,
Erhebungen
firmness Festigkeit
first floor (AE)
Erdgeschoß (USA)
flux Fluß

GLOSSARY

fly into a fit of rage Wutanfall bekommen
for our part was uns betrifft
form Formblatt, Formular
fox; an old ~ ein alter Fuchs
French fries Pommes frites
frequent-flyer Vielflieger
from the macro to the micro vom Allgemeinen zum Besonderen
frown die Stirn runzeln
fund finanzieren
funeral Beerdigung
furnish someone with jemanden beliefern, versorgen mit
fuzz Flausen, Firlefanz

gadget Gerät
Gaelic gälisch (keltisch)
gap Lücke
gather information Informationen sammeln
gear Ausrüstung
gents (AE) meine Herren
get one's figures wrong mit falschen Zahlen arbeiten
get into something sich anfreunden mit
get hot about sich über etwas aufregen
get the hang of kapieren
gift Geschenk
go for zugreifen, akzeptieren
go to the polls zur Wahlurne gehen
goal Ziel
good value for money preiswert
good loser guter Verlierer
good health auf Ihre Gesundheit
goodies Bonbons, klasse Sachen
gradually nach und nach
grains of truth Körner der Wahrheit
grant gewähren
grease someone's palm jemanden bestechen
greenback Dollar
grey matter graue Zellen (Gehirn)
grip Griff
guess meinen, raten
guidelines Richtlinien

habit Gewohnheit
hacked from the same rock as aus dem gleichen Holz geschnitzt wie
hairy haarig
handle Griff
handle bars Lenkrad
hankering for vodka Hang zum, Vorliebe für Wodka
hassle; no ~ (AE) kein Problem
have a bad press keine gute Presse haben
have in common etwas gemeinsam haben
head of purchasing Einkaufsleiter
headmaster Schuldirektor
heart beat Herzschlag
hidebound engstirnig, beschränkt, borniert
hilly landscape hügelige Landschaft
hit it off with sich gut verstehen mit
hit the bull's eye den Nagel auf den Kopf treffen; einen Treffer landen
hit the brakes auf die Bremse treten
honesty Ehrlichkeit
honored; I'm ~ to meet you es ist mir eine Ehre, Sie kennenzulernen
honour (v.) ehren
hospitality Gastfreundschaft
host country Gastland
hostess Gastgeberin
how does that grab you? wie gefällt Ihnen das?
hug umarmen, drücken
humble bescheiden, demütig
humble; our ~ selves unsere Wenigkeiten
humiliate erniedrigen, demütigen

GLOSSARY

I sincerely hope ich hoffe aufrichtig, daß ...
I'm hooked on these things ich bin scharf auf so was
Iberian Peninsula Iberische Halbinsel
idiocy Irrsinn; Torheit
imminent; an ~ meeting ein bevorstehendes Treffen
impatient ungeduldig
implementation Durchführung, Umsetzung
implement improvements Verbesserungen einbauen
implication Auswirkung, Folge
improper dress unschickliche Kleidung
improve verbessern
in the long term langfristig, auf lange Sicht
in charge of verantwortlich für, leiten
in all respects in jeder Hinsicht
inadvertence Unachtsamkeit
inanimate elements nicht lebende Dinge
include umfassen, einschließen
income Einkommen
incomprehensible unverständlich
independent unabhängig
inequality Ungleichheit
inexperienced unerfahren
initial draft erster Entwurf
initiate beginnen, initiieren
inquiry Befragung
instructions Anweisungen
insubordination Ungehorsam
insurance Versicherung
intend beabsichtigen
intense peak hoher Grad, Spitzenwert
intent Absicht
interfere with stören
interpreter Dolmetscher
intersection (AE) Kreuzung (USA)
invader Eindringling
invoice (n.; v.) Rechnung; berechnen
involved; be ~ beteiligt sein
involved; how long have you been ~ ? wie lange sind Sie schon dabei?
irrepressibly unverwüstlich, nicht unterzukriegen
irritating ärgerlich, lästig,
it's a long stint es ist eine lange Zeit
items Artikel, Punkte

job description Arbeitsplatzbeschreibung
jump the queue sich vordrängen

keen; be ~ on scharf sein auf
kidding; be ~ Spaß machen
kidney Niere
kindness Freundlichkeit
knighthood Adelstitel

l'érudit (franz.) Gelehrter
lack of respect Respektlosigkeit
lack; ~ patience keine Geduld haben
land the contract einen Vertrag an Land ziehen
latest; the ~ joke der neueste Witz
launch auf den Markt bringen
lazy faul
leading economic power führende Wirtschaftsmacht
lean companies verschlankte Firmen
leisure facilities Freizeiteinrichtungen
let off steam Dampf ablassen
let's get to the point kommen wir zur Sache
liar Lügner
light a stadium ein Stadion beleuchten
lighter leichter
line hier: Sortiment, Reihe

GLOSSARY

loathing Abscheu
located gelegen
lock onto (Ziel) erfassen und verfolgen
lodge unterbringen
lofty heights erhabene Höhen
loisirs (franz.) Freizeit
look forward to sich freuen auf
loot Beute; hier: Kies, Knete
lose control of one's temper die Kontrolle über sich verlieren

machine something herstellen, be-, verarbeiten
mainland Festland
major airport wichtiger Flughafen
majority shareholder Hauptaktionär
make something hum in Schwung bringen
make no distinction keinen Unterschied machen
managerial position leitende Stellung
manners Manieren, Benehmen
manufacturing plant Produktionsstätte, Fabrik
market research Marktforschung
market leader Marktführer
market potential Marktchancen; Marktpotential

master the language die Sprache beherrschen
matter; to the ~ zur Sache
matters physical materielle Dinge
measurement Maß, Maßeinheit
mechanical legs künstliche Beine
Mediterranean Mittelmeer-
medium-sized companies mittelständische Betriebe
meet someone halfway jemandem auf halbem Wege entgegenkommen
meet someone's expectations jemandes Erwartungen erfüllen
member of the board Vorstandsmitglied
menu Speisekarte
meritocracy Leistungsgesellschaft
mining Bergbau
minutes Protokoll
modest bescheiden
modesty Bescheidenheit
monkeys' brains Affenhirn
mono-tasking; be ~ eine Aufgabe beenden, bevor man die nächste in Angriff nimmt
move; thinking several ~s ahead mehrere Züge vorausdenken
muddle through sich durchwursteln

multi-tasking; be ~ mit mehreren Aufgaben gleichzeitig beschäftigt
mumbling Gemurmel
muscularity Muskelkraft, muskulöse Statur
musical chairs die Reise nach Jerusalem
mutual trust gegenseitiges Vertrauen

national anthem Nationalhymne
national level campaign landesweiter Feldzug
native Eingeborener
negotiate verhandeln
negotiation Verhandlung
negotiator Unterhändler, Verhandlungsführer
nervous breakdown Nervenzusammenbruch
no big deal nichts Besonderes
nod nicken
notice; give proper ~ fristgerecht kündigen
novelty Neuheit

oaken barrel Eichenfaß
obey gehorchen
objective (n.) Ziel
obliged; be ~ to consider something etwas überdenken müssen

GLOSSARY

obtain better terms bessere Bedingungen aushandeln
obviously offensichtlich
occupation hier: Besatzung
odd sonderbar
off the coast of America vor der Küste von Amerika
offend beleidigen
offended; be ~ beleidigt sein
offending car hier: Unfallverursacher
offensive beleidigend
old-fashioned altmodisch
operation Unternehmen; Firma
opposite Gegenteil
oral agreement mündliche Vereinbarung
origin Ursprung, Herkunft
outbreaks of temper Gefühlsausbrüche
outline a position eine Position umreißen
overjoyed überglücklich
overview Überblick
overwhelm überwältigen
owl Eule
owner Besitzer
oysters Austern

pager Piepser
pale; go ~ blaß werden
pant suit Hosenanzug
parentage Abstammung
part friends als Freunde auseinandergehen
participant Teilnehmer
pass a law ein Gesetz verabschieden
pastime Freizeitbeschäftigung
patron saint Schutzheiliger
pattern Struktur, Muster
peak hours Stoßzeiten
permission Erlaubnis
personal goals persönliche Ziele
persuade überreden
photograph display Fotorahmen
physical contact Körperkontakt
pick someone up jemanden abholen, auflesen
pile Haufen
pipe forth music Musik erklingen lassen
place principles above money Prinzipien über Geld stellen
plaice Scholle
pontificate dogmatisch sein; predigen
praise (n.;v.) Lob; loben
prefer vorziehen, lieber tun
preferably vorzugsweise, am liebsten
pregnancy Schwangerschaft
prejudice Vorurteil
present company excepted Anwesende ausgenommen
preserve their language die Sprache bewahren
prevent embarrassment Peinlichkeiten vermeiden

previously agreed terms zuvor vereinbarte Bedingungen
primary object vorrangiges Ziel
prints Druckerzeugnisse
proceed to begeben Sie sich zu, nach
product range Produktpalette
proportion Anteil
proposal Vorschlag
proprietor Eigentümer
prosecute gerichtlich verfolgen
prospect Kunde
prosper gedeihen
proud; be ~ of stolz sein auf
provide someone with trainers jemanden mit Lehrern versorgen
pump someone's hand jemandes Hand lange und kräftig schütteln
punctual pünktlich
punctuality Pünktlichkeit
purchase Einkauf
pushy aufdringlich, drängelnd, aggressiv
put into practice in die Praxis umsetzen

question the authority die Autorität in Frage stellen
queue Warteschlange
quid Pfundnote
quotation Angebot; Zitat

GLOSSARY

quote hier: ein Angebot machen

racket ball amerikanische Sportart, ähnlich wie Squash
raise something etwas heben, erhöhen
Ramadan Fastenzeit
rank Rang, Stellung,
rear lights Rücklichter
receipt Quittung
receive information Informationen empfangen
recently kürzlich
reckon der Meinung sein
recline zurückbeugen, -lehnen
recommend empfehlen
recreation facilities Erholungseinrichtungen
red tape Bürokratie, Papierkram
reduce the length by ... um ... verkürzen
refer to verweisen, sich beziehen auf
referee Schiedsrichter; Berichterstatter
reference; for later ~ hier: für späteren Gebrauch
reflect widerspiegeln
refuse a suggestion einen Vorschlag ablehnen
refuse food Essen ablehnen
regard; have high ~ for Hochachtung haben vor
regulars Stammkunden
regulations Vorschriften

relate to someone hier: mit jemandem reden
relatively speaking hier: mehr oder weniger
reliability Zuverlässigkeit
remedy (Heil-) Mittel
remove entfernen, wegnehmen
renegotiate neu verhandeln
replace the pin Stift ersetzen
reply (n.;v.) Antwort; antworten
reputation Ruf
required; be ~ to know wissen müssen
requirements Anforderungen, Bedürfnisse
research Forschung, Untersuchung
reservations hier: Vorbehalte
responsibility Verantwortung
responsible for verantwortlich für
retired party officials pensionierte Parteifunktionäre
return toasts Trinksprüche erwidern
revenue Einkommen
reverse rückgängig machen
reward Belohnung
Right on target! Ins Schwarze getroffen!
rip-off Wucher
rock the boat die Sache gefährden
rod Rute
roll Semmel, Brötchen
rude grob, unhöflich
rustle up auftreiben

sake; for the ~ of discussion um der Diskussion willen
sale Verkauf
sales argument Verkaufsargument
sales call Verkaufsgespräch, -besuch
sample Warenmuster
say provocative things provokante Dinge sagen
scholar Gelehrter
scholarly learner akademischer Schüler
schoolmate Schulkamerad
scone Teegebäck
score Erfolg haben, Treffer erzielen
score points Punkte sammeln
scraggy mager, dürr
search for something nach etwas suchen
search one's soul seine Seele erforschen
see ya bis dann, auf bald
self-assured selbstsicher
self-confidence Selbstvertrauen
senses Sinne, Verstand
seriousness Ernsthaftigkeit
settle details Einzelheiten regeln
settle something on the phone etwas per Telefon regeln
shaft of the club Stiel des Golfschlägers

GLOSSARY

share someone's opinion jemandes Meinung teilen
Shoot! Schieß los!
shrewd scharfsinnig, gescheit
shut up den Mund halten
sign of confidence Zeichen des Vertrauens
signature Unterschrift
silence Stille, Schweigen
similar ähnlich
since hier: da, weil
sirloin steak Lendensteak
site Gelände, Grundstück, Anlage
size Umfang, Größe
skilled geschickt, geübt
slap someone on the shoulder jemandem auf die Schulter hauen
slip (in terminology) sich versprechen
slow on the uptake schwer von Begriff
smart schlau, klug
smooth glatt, sanft
snakes Schlangen
social occasion gesellschaftliches Ereignis
soften mildern, abschwächen
sole Sohle
sophisticated kultiviert, raffiniert, hochstehend
sound; that ~s good gut klingen
sphere Kugel
split hairs Haare spalten
square spießig, altmodisch

stable Stall
stand out from the rest sich von allen anderen abheben
standards; by American ~ für amerikanische Verhältnisse
starters Vorspeisen
startling hier: verblüffend
starvation hier: Hungerkuren
status-conscious statusbewußt
step by step Schritt für Schritt
stick to sich halten an
stimulate business das Geschäft beleben
stipulate even the smallest details selbst die kleinsten Details festlegen, vereinbaren
straight into the rough direkt ins Gebüsch
straightforward offen, direkt, unkompliziert
strike (struck, struck) against schlagen gegen
strike a balance Mittelweg finden
stringing system Bespannung (des Schlägers)
structures Gebäude
subordinate Untergebener
subsidiary Tochtergesellschaft
subsystem Untersystem
subtlety Feinheit, Spitzfindigkeit
successful erfolgreich
suggest vorschlagen
suitcase Koffer
superficial oberflächlich

superior hier: überheblich
superior; be ~ to someone jemandem überlegen sein
supply liefern
supply and demand Angebot und Nachfrage
support a suggestion einen Vorschlag unterstützen
support; give ~ to someone jemanden unterstützen
suppose; I ~ ich nehme an, ich vermute
surprise someone jemanden überraschen
survive überleben
suspicion Verdacht, Argwohn
suspicious argwöhnisch; verdächtig
swallow the ultimatum das Ultimatum schlucken
swallow schlucken

tactile tastbar, fühlbar
take for granted für selbstverständlich halten
take something at face value etwas für bare Münze nehmen
take responsibility Verantwortung übernehmen
take advantage of something etwas ausnützen

GLOSSARY

take it seriously es ernst nehmen
take into account in Betracht ziehen, berücksichtigen
take up business Geschäftsbeziehungen aufnehmen
talk feelings Gefühle ansprechen
talk tough zäh verhandeln
target a campaign eine Kampagne ausrichten auf
target; be right on target den Nagel auf den Kopf treffen
taste schmecken, kosten
tax-free allowances zollfreie Mengen
tear down (tore, torn) abreißen
tee off (v.) abschlagen (beim Golf)
teetotaller Abstinenzler
temperamental reizbar, leicht erregbar
tense angespannt, nervös
that'll fix him up das bringt ihn wieder auf die Beine
that's a bit over the top das geht etwas zu weit
that's where it's at das ist der springende Punkt
the anger of the golfer reaches mercurial heights der Golfspieler bekommt einen Jähzornanfall
think straight klar denken

thoroughly gründlich
threaten drohen
throw one's ace down seinen Trumpf ausspielen
throwaways hier: Scheinbedingungen
tie Krawatte
ties; family ~ Familienbande
tip Trinkgeld geben
tool Instrument, Werkzeug
top; be on ~ of the situation über der Situation stehen
touchy ; be ~ about empfindlich gegen
tough zäh
tough talk robuste Sprache
towel Handtuch
trade-unions Gewerkschaften
trader Händler
traffic police Verkehrspolizei
transmitter Sender
tremendous riesig
trickle Rinnsal
trunk (BE: boot) Kofferraum
trust Vertrauen
trustworthy vertrauenswürdig
truth Wahrheit
turnover Umsatz
two-stroke motor Zweitaktmotor

unattended unbeaufsichtigt
undersized zu klein

unfamiliar meals ungewohnte Mahlzeiten
unforeseen circumstances unvorhergesehene Umstände
university degrees akademische Abschlüsse
unreliable unzuverlässig
unseemly ungehörig
unsuitable unpassend, ungeeignet
untrustworthy unzuverlässig
Up the Basques! Es leben die Basken!
up to now bis jetzt, soweit
up-market segment Marktsegment am oberen Ende der Preisskala
upset; get ~ sich beunruhigen, aufregen
urge to win Trieb zu gewinnen
used; be ~ to gewöhnt sein an
USP (unique selling point) einzigartiges Verkaufsargument

valuable wertvoll
values Werte
variety Vielfalt
VAT (value added tax) Mehrwertsteuer
vein of gold Goldader
victory Sieg
violate a comandment gegen ein Gebot verstoßen

GLOSSARY

violent heftig, gewalttätig
virtue Tugend
visual bildhaft
vital documents lebenswichtige Dokumente
vitally important lebenswichtig, sehr wichtig
vivid lebhaft
vociferously lautstark, schreiend
vous vous êtes trompé de porte Sie haben sich in der Tür geirrt
vowel Vokal

wait in line in der Schlange warten
waitress Kellnerin
watertight conditions hieb- und stichfeste Bedingungen
weapon Waffe
weary walker müder Wanderer
weight Gewicht
weird verrückt, schrullig, sonderbar
wham, bam, thank you, ma'am hier: und da haben Sie den Salat
wheels of commerce Räderwerk des Handels
whistle-stop tour Reise von Ort zu Ort
wide spread weitverbreitet
wisecrack Witzelei
with a view to mit Aussicht auf
without doubt zweifelsohne
work ethic Arbeitsethik, -moral
wrestler Ringkämpfer
wrist-band Armband

your hair'll stand on end die Haare werden dir zu Berge stehen

SOURCES

Lynne Brennan, David Block *The Complete Book of Business Etiquette. The Essential Guide to Getting Ahead in Business.* Piatkus: London, 1991.

Paul Gibbs *Euro-Management.* Geschäftskultur, Marketingstrategien, Verbrauchertrends. Ullstein: Frankfurt, 1995.

Lennie Copeland, Lewis Griggs *Going International. How to make friends and deal effectively in the global marketplace.* New American Library: New York, 1986.

James Davidson, Neil Shand *James Davidson's True Brit.* Arrow Books: London, 1992.

Drew Launay *The Xenophobe's guide to the Spanish.* Ravette Books: Horsham, 1993.

Richard D. Lewis *When Cultures Collide. Managing successfully across cultures.* Nicholas Brealy Publishing: London, 1996.

Georges Mikes *The Best of Mikes.* Pan Books: London, 1962.

Antony Miall *The Xenophobe's guide to the English.* Ravette Books: Horsham, 1993.

John Mole *Mind Your Manners. Managing business cultures in Europe.* N. Brealy Publishing: London, 1996.

Nick Yapp, Michael Syrett *The Xenophobe's guide to the French.* Ravette Books: Horsham, 1993.

Stefan Zeidenitz, Ben Barkow *The Xenophobe's guide to the Germans.* Ravette Books: Horsham, 1993.

Business English

Der Text-Trainer für Windows

Ein Sprach-Lernprogramm
von R. Kleinschroth und W. Bessler

- Wortschatzerklärung und Grammatikregeln per Mausklick
- Wortschatz üben Sie mit dem integrierten Vokabeltrainer
- Sie lernen und üben die Grammatik zu den Texten mit den *Grammar Rhymes* und *Grammar Jokes* des Grammatiktrainers
- Sie rekonstruieren die Texte mit dem Lückentextgenerator
- Das Übersetzen üben Sie mit dem Übersetzungstrainer
- Wortschatz, Grammatik und Lücken- und Übersetzungstests können Sie auch ausdrucken
- Der Text-Trainer ist ein Autorenprogramm. Sie können eigene Lektionen für sich und andere erstellen und diese vertonen.

Systemanforderungen: Windows 3.1 oder höher,
1,44 MB Diskettenlaufwerk;
2 MB Arbeitsspeicher; 10 MB freier Festplattenspeicher

Robert Kleinschroth
Richard-Kuhn-Str. 39
69123 Heidelberg

Ich bestelle den Texttrainer Version 1.2 zum Preis von **DM 79**

Zahlungsart:
☐ Scheck liegt bei
☐ Bezahlung gegen Rechnung
☐ Ich zahle per Überweisung Konto Nr.: 30 389 603
   BLZ: 672 900 00 bei der Heidelberger Volksbank

Vorname, Name: ....
Straße: ....
PLZ, Ort: ....
Datum: .... **Unterschrift:** ....

Train Your Business English!

**A. A Book a seminar!
Get on top of Cross-cultural differences.**

**B. Train your presentations and
meetings skills
with the author.**

**Seminars customised for you
and your company**

For details contact:

Dr. René Bosewitz
PELC Seminar
Belfortstr. 1
69115 Heidelberg
Tel 0 62 21 / 2 75 90
Fax 0 62 21 / 2 75 13

Business English

Geschäftsbesuche, Briefe, Verträge, Telefonenglisch, Mitarbeitergespräche, Verhandlungen mit Lieferanten, aber auch Konferenzen und Auftritte auf Kongressen verlangen ein klares sprachliches Konzept: Die Bücher von **René Bosewitz** und **Robert Kleinschroth** helfen in allen beruflichen Standardsituationen.

Check Your Language Level
Business English auf dem Prüfstand
(rororo sprachen 60268 / Oktober 1997)

Manage in English *Business English rund um die Firma*
(rororo sprachen 60137)
Lockere Texte, ironische Dialoge, geistreiche Zitate von Konfuzius bis Murphy und Witze über Pleiten, Pech und Pannen im Geschäftsleben vermitteln Know-how, Wortschatz, Idioms und Redemittel zugleich.

How to Phone Effectively
Business English am Telefon
(rororo sprachen 60139 /
Buch mit Audio-CD
rororo sprachen 60146 /
Toncassette
rororo sprachen 60147)
Das Buch vermittelt mit das notwendige Telefonenglisch in typischen Situationen. Wie beginnt man ein Gespräch, wie bricht man es ab, wie bremst man einen Schnellredner, wie verschafft man sich Gewißheit. Die Toncassette zum Buch oder die Audio-CD im Buch verrät, wie sich das alles anhört, und schult im Sprechen.

Better than the Boss *Business English fürs Büro*
(rororo sprachen 60138)

Test Your Management Skills
Business English für Durchstarter
(rororo sprachen 60260)
Aktive und zukünftige Manager lernen die Fährnisse des Berufslebens besser zu umsteuern und sich im internationalen Business sprachlich zu behaupten.

Drop Them a Line *Business English im Schriftverkehr*
(rororo sprachen 60261)

Get Through at Meetings
Business English für Konferenzen und Präsentationen
(rororo sprachen 60262 /
mit Audio-CD
rororo sprachen 60265 /
Toncassette
rororo sprachen 60266)

Bryan Hemming
Business English from A to Z
Wörter und Wendungen für alle Situationen
(rororo sprachen 60269 /
November 1997)

rororo sachbuch

Englisch

Gunther Bischoff
Speak you English?
*Programmierte Übung
zum Verlernen typisch
deutscher Englischfehler*
(rororo 16857)

Hartmut Breitkreuz
False Friends *Stolpersteine
des deutsch-englischen
Wortschatzes*
(rororo 18492)
More False Friends
*Tückische Fallen des
deutsch-englischen
Wortschatzes*
(rororo 19172)

Hartmut Breitkreuz /
René Bosewitz
Do up your Phrasals *500
Wendungen wichtiger
Verben*
(rororo 18344)
**Getting on Top of Idiomatic
Verbs** *Tausend Wendungen
im Kontext*
(rororo 18523)

Ian Galbraith / Paul Krieger
Englisch in letzter Minute
(Buch: rororo 19630, Buch
mit Cassette: rororo 19631,
Cassette: rororo 19704)

Hans-Georg Heuber
**Talk one's head off. Ein Loch in
den Bauch reden** *Englische
Redewendungen und ihre
deutschen «opposite
numbers»*
(rororo 17653)

Uwe Kreisel /
Pamela Ann Tabbert
English One *Englisch reden
und verstehen.
Ein Grundkurs*
(Buch: rororo 19180,
Cassette: rororo 19181)

English Two *Englisch reden
und verstehen.
Ein Aufbaukurs*
(Buch: rororo 19320,
Cassette: 19321)
Ultimate Idioms *Der Schlüssel
zu den britischen und
amerikanischen Redewen-
dungen*
(rororo 18492)

Paul Krieger
Supertrain Grammar *Der
direkte Weg zu englischer
Grammatik*
(rororo 60107)

Ernest Pasakarnis
Master your Idioms *Der
Schlüssel zu den englischen
Redewendungen*
(rororo 18491)

Emer O'Sullivan /
Dietmar Rösler
Modern Talking *Englisches
Quasselbuch mit Sprüchen
und Widersprüchen*
(rororo sprachen 18427)

rororo sprachen

Französisch

Französisch lernen: alltagsnah und von Anfang an. Für das Lernen allein oder in der Gruppe.

Claire Bretécher / Isabelle Jue / Nicole Zimmermannn
Le Français avec les Frustrés
Ein Comic-Sprachhelfer
(rororo 18423)

Armelle Damblemont / Petra Preßmar
Français Un *Französisch reden und verstehen. Ein Grundkurs*
(Buch: rororo 19106, Cassette: rororo 19107)

Isabelle Jue / Nicole Zimmermann
Français Deux *Französisch reden und verstehen. Ein Aufbaukurs*
(Buch: rororo 19311, Cassette: rororo 19312)
Französisch in letzter Minute
(Buch: rororo 19628, Buch mit Cassette: rororo 19629, Cassette: rororo 19702)

Ahmed Haddedou
Questions grammaticales de A à Z *Tout ce que vous avez toujours voulu savoir sur la grammaire sans jamais oser le demander*
(rororo 18445)

Robert Kleinschroth
La Conversation en s'amusant *Sprechsituationen mit Witz gemeistert*
(rororo 18873)

Robert Kleinschroth / Dieter Maupel
La Grammaire en s'amusant *Wichtige Regeln zum Anlachen*
(rororo sprachen 18714)

Marie-Thérèse Pignolo / Hans-Georg Heuber
Ne mâche pas tes mots *Nimm kein Blatt vor den Mund! Französische Redewendungen und ihre deutschen Pendants*
(rororo 17472)

Jacques Soussan
Pouvez-vous Français?
Programm zum Verlernen typisch deutscher Französischfehler
(rororo 16940)

rororo sprachen

rororo sprachen wird herausgegeben von Ludwig Moos. Ein Gesamtverzeichnis der Reihe finden Sie in der *Rowohlt Revue*. Vierteljährlich neu. Kostenlos in Ihrer Buchhandlung.

Überflieger

Die «Überflieger» sind der Einstieg für alle, denen ein ganzes Lehrbuch zu langwierig und ein Sprachführer zu wörterbuchhaft ist. Schon in wenigen Tagen kann man damit die notwendigen Grundkenntnisse erwerben, um sich in einem fremden Land zu verständigen. Damit Urlaub und Geschäftsreise nicht nur sprachlich ein voller Erfolg werden, gibt es außerdem praktische Tips zu Kultur und Alltag.
Eine Auswahl der lieferbaren Titel:

Uwe Kreisel /
Pamela Ann Tabbert
American Slang in letzter Minute
(Buch: rororo 19623, Buch mit Cassette: rororo 19624, Cassette: rororo 19705)

Hanne Schönig /
Hatem Lahmar
Arabisch in letzter Minute
(Buch: rororo 19541, Buch mit Cassette: rororo 19542, Cassette: rororo 19700)

Petra Schaeber
Bralilianisch in letzter Minute
(Buch: rororo 19977, Buch mit Cassette: rororo 19979, Cassette: 19978)

Isabelle Jue /
Nicole Zimmermann
Französisch in letzter Minute
(Buch: rororo 19628, Buch mit Cassette: rororo 19629, Cassette: rororo 19702)

Frida Bordon /
Giuseppe Siciliano
Italienisch in letzter Minute
(Buch: rororo 19626, Buch mit Cassette: rororo 19627, Cassette: rororo 19703)

Elisabeth Völpel
Portugiesisch in letzter Minute
(Buch: rororo 19686, Buch mit Cassette: rororo 19687, Cassette: rororo 19736)

Dorothee Bernhardt
Russisch in letzter Minute
(Buch: rororo 19797, Buch mit Cassette: rororo 19799, Cassette: rororo 19798)

Christof Kehr
Spanisch in letzter Minute
(Buch: rororo 19526, Buch mit Cassette: rororo 19527, Cassette: rororo 19701)

Karl-Heinz Scheffler
Türkisch in letzter Minute
(Buch: rororo 19688, Buch mit Cassette: rororo 19689, Cassette: rororo 19735)

rororo sprachen

rororo sprachen wird herausgegeben von Ludwig Moos. Ein Gesamtverzeichnis der Reihe finden Sie in der *Rowohlt Revue*. Vierteljährlich neu. Kostenlos in Ihrer Buchhandlung.